YORK N

General Editors: Profe.
of Stirling) & Professor Suheil Bushrui (*American University of Beirut*)

George Eliot

MIDDLEMARCH

Notes by Anna Rutherford

A MUS A (NSW CONSERVATORIUM OF MUSIC)
BA (NEWCASTLE, NSW)
Head of the Department of Commonwealth Literature, University of Aarhus

LONGMAN
YORK PRESS

YORK PRESS
Immeuble Esseily, Place Riad Solh, Beirut.

LONGMAN GROUP LIMITED
Longman House, Burnt Mill, Harlow,
Essex CM20 2JE, England
Associated companies, branches and representatives
throughout the world

First published 1985
Eighth impression 1994

ISBN 0-582-03087-0

Produced by Longman Singapore Publishers Pte Ltd
Printed in Singapore

Contents

Contents

Part 1

Introduction

The life of George Eliot

George Eliot, whose real name was Mary Ann Evans, was born at Arbury Farm near Nuneaton in Warwickshire on 22 November 1819. She was the third child of Robert and Christiana Evans.

Robert Evans was a land agent and managed the estate of Francis Newdigate. When Mary Ann was four months old the family moved to another house on the estate. This was Griff House. It was situated in a very beautiful and quiet agricultural area much like the Raveloe of *Silas Marner*, yet not too far away was the beginning of an industrialised area similar to the one from which Silas Marner came. Her early life here was to play a vital role for it meant that many years later when she chose a rural setting for certain of her novels, namely *Silas Marner*, *The Mill on the Floss* and *Adam Bede*, George Eliot was able to draw on her childhood memories.

With her brother Isaac, of whom she was very fond, Mary Ann first of all attended Mrs Moore's dame school, but when she was only five she was sent to Miss Lathom's boarding school at Attleborough. Needless to say she was lonely and homesick and longed for holidays when she could be with her father and brother.

In 1828 Mary Ann changed schools. The principal of her new school was Maria Lewis, a believer in evangelical Christianity. She had a strong influence on Mary Ann, who became much more religiously fervent and conservative than the rest of her family who were conventional Anglicans.

In 1832, when she was thirteen, Mary Ann once more changed schools, for it was felt that she had learned all she could from Miss Lewis's school. This time she went to a school in Coventry run by Mary and Rebecca Franklin, daughters of Francis Franklin, the Minister of Cow Lane Baptist Chapel. Mary Ann's religious fervour was increased, she became more non-conformist and adopted the Calvinism of the the Franklins. To show that she had renounced the world she took to wearing an extremely unbecoming cap on her head to make herself ugly. This was hardly necessary, for everyone, including Mary Ann herself, knew she was already ugly. Years later it was thought by many that she would marry Herbert Spencer (1820–1903), the famous social philosopher, but Spencer declared that even though he found Marian, as she was then called, 'the most admirable woman mentally' he had ever met, he did not want to marry her because of her lack of beauty. He was in love with her, he said, but her long nose made her difficult to kiss. George Eliot's ugliness was a point of discussion for many. Another famous writer, Henry James (1843–1916) described her as 'magnificently ugly—deliciously hideous'. Her face was often compared to that of a horse and perhaps the unkindest description of all was when she was likened to 'an elderly Jewish cab-horse with ringlets'.

In 1836 Mary Ann's mother died and she was forced to leave school and look after her father and brother. At school Mary Ann had excelled at her lessons, particularly French, German, music and English composition. She continued with her studies at home, reading Italian, Greek and Latin, as well as German and French. In matters of religion she became even more devout and narrow-minded. She looked upon any entertainment as sinful and refused to accompany her brother to the theatre when they went to London. She herself later described this period as one when she used 'to go about like an owl'.

Another move was made in 1841 when she went with her father to live in Coventry. Mary Ann had continued to read widely and deeply, especially in the new philosophy and theology. This reading, and the influence of a new group of liberal friends in Coventry, especially Charles Bray, caused her to abandon her previous religious views. The entry in Robert Evans's diary for Sunday, 2 January reads, 'Went to Trinity Church in the forenoon . . . Mary Ann did not go'. Her father refused to live with her if she would not go to church and for three weeks she stayed with her brother. Mary Ann then returned to her father's house and agreed to attend church with him, but she continued to reject all religious dogmas and remained an agnostic until her death.

Despite her rejection of traditional Christianity she retained her interest in theology and her first published work was a translation of David Friedrich Strauss's (1808–74) *Leben Jesu* (1835) (*The Life of Christ* in translated version, 1846). After the death of her father she went abroad for a certain period with the Brays, then she settled in London, where she became assistant editor of the *Westminster Review*, a liberal, intellectual periodical edited by John Chapman.

In London Marian, as she now called herself, was to meet the most brilliant writers and thinkers of the age, including Charles Dickens (1812–70), W. M. Thackeray, (1811–63), Lord Tennyson (1809–92), Thomas Carlyle (1795–1881), Charles Darwin (1809–82), and Herbert Spencer (1820–1903). Among them was George Henry Lewes (1817–78); he and Marian fell in love. Lewes was already married and although his wife had deserted him he was unable to get a divorce. Marian made up her mind that although she could not be legally married to George Lewes she would live with him as his wife. Her decision to do so was a very brave one for such things were not done in that age.

The typical reaction to what she and George Lewes did can be found in a letter from the sculptor Thomas Woolner (1826–92) to the painter William Bell Scott (1811–90). He asks Scott if he has heard what has happened and, in case he hasn't, tells him '[that] blackguard Lewes has bolted with a — and is living in Germany with her . . . I will not further lift the mantle and display the filthy contamination of these hideous satyrs and smirking moralists . . . stink pots of humanity'. 'Stink pots of humanity'. Mary Ann knew that this was the abuse that would be hurled at her but she decided to go ahead with something she did not believe was wrong. As Lord Acton (1834–1902) remarked, 'The sanctions of religion were indifferent to her after rejecting its doctrines and also, granted sufficient cause, she was prepared to disregard the social law of England.' It is ironical that Queen Victoria (1837–1901) gave her name to an age that is renowned for its narrowness, prudery and hypocrisy, yet she did not condemn George Eliot and her relationship with George Lewes. In a letter to her daughter Queen Victoria discussed liaisons where 'the outward earthly form cannot be given by man! In God's eyes,' the Queen wrote, 'I believe, as surely as I write this, that this will be considered as holy and right.' So did George Eliot! In a letter to Vincent Holbeche, her solicitor, she wrote, 'Our marriage is not a legal one, though it is regarded by us both as a sacred bond.'

In 1854 she and George Lewes went to Germany together and on their return lived happily as husband and wife until George Lewes's death in 1878. At first they were social outcasts, except amongst their free-thinking liberal friends, but eventually their relationship was accepted by all except a few. These included Marian's brother Isaac, who did not write to her for twenty-three years, the time she lived with George Lewes. A short while after George Lewes died Marian married John Cross but only eight months after they were married she died, on 22 December 1880.

George Eliot's literary career

Marian Evans had thought of herself as a critic and translator. It was George Lewes who persuaded her that her real gift lay in writing fiction and he encouraged her to do so. In 1857 her first story was puiblished in•*Blackwood's Magazine.* Two other stories appeared in the same magazine and in 1858 the three were published in book form under the title *Scenes of Clerical Life.*

From the beginning Marian Evans wrote under the pseudonym of

George Eliot, George because it was Lewes's name and Eliot because she liked the sound, 'a good mouth-filling word,' she said, 'easily pronounced'. Why did she decide to write under another name? Several suggestions have been put forward, all of which no doubt contain some degree of truth. First of all Marian Evans had thought of herself as a critic and she feared that people might disregard her criticism if they knew she wrote novels. The second reason, and most probably the major one, was the fear that people would refuse to buy the book of a woman living with a man to whom she was not married. She had good reason to believe this. People who had praised her work condemned it when they discovered that she was the author. Finally, and this was the reason for choosing a man's name, she wanted her books judged on their own merits and 'not', George Lewes said, 'prejudged as the work of a woman'.

Whilst people could not recognise the author they could recognise the talent of the writer. Her first book was the beginning of a success story that was to reach its highest peak on the publication of *Middlemarch* in 1871. This work was described then, and still is, as a 'masterpiece'. It was considered to be George Eliot's finest novel and she in turn was regarded as England's greatest living novelist, Dickens having died in 1870.

During her lifetime she enjoyed a very high reputation, but after her death there was a decline. The post-Victorian critics, in rejecting the narrow moral codes of the Victorian period, also rejected George Eliot's novels. What they failed to realise was that when she philosophised or made a moral judgement it was not based on any particular unchanging religious or social dogma. These she regarded as instruments of torture that 'rack and stretch' the soul. 'My function,' George Eliot said, 'is that of the *aesthetic*, not the doctrinal teacher—the rousing of nobler emotions, which mankind desire the social right, not the prescribing, of special measures.' The doctrine she believed in, and preached in her novels, was that of meliorism, a belief which affirms that the world may be made better by human effort. In his book *Religious Humanism and the Victorian Novel*, V. C. Knoepflmacher recounts that in 1853 Marian Evans told herself in a rare outburst of confidence: 'Heaven help us! said the old religions—the new one, from its very lack of that faith, will teach us all the more to help one another'. Nothing could be more radical than that; her religion was a socialist one of love, duty and self-sacrifice for the happiness of her fellow human beings on this earth.

It took the next generation of critics to realise this. The 1920s brought about a renewed interest in her novels. One of the persons responsible for this was another major English female novelist, Virginia Woolf (1882–1941). George Eliot's reputation has continued to increase. She was one of the few novelists that F. R. Leavis (1895–1978) included in his major work of criticism on the novel, *The Great Tradition* (1948), and today she is still quite rightly regarded as one of the greatest of the English novelists.

A note on the text

The edition of *Middlemarch* used for these Notes is the Penguin English Library edition, edited by W. J. Harvey, Penguin Books, Harmondsworth, 1965. This text is based upon that of the one-volume edition of *Middlemarch* published in 1874. For a discussion of the origin and composition of *Middlemarch* see Part 3 of these Notes.

Part 2

Summaries
of MIDDLEMARCH

A general summary

Book One

Dorothea and her younger sister, Celia, are orphans and live with their
uncle, Mr Brooke, at his home, Tipton Grange. One evening Mr
Brooke gives a dinner party to which he invites Sir James Chettam and
the Reverend Mr Casaubon. Sir James hopes to marry Dorothea but
Dorothea, who has intellectual ambitions, prefers the much older and
more scholarly Mr Casaubon. He is looking for a wife who will tend
him in his old age, believes that Dorothea will prove suitable and
proposes to her. Much to everyone's horror Dorothea accepts him.

One of the people most upset about the marriage is Mrs
Cadwallader, the rector's wife. She had planned that Dorothea marry
Sir James but she now advises him to turn to Celia which he does
though his pride is hurt. This pleases Dorothea as she has a scheme to
build some cottages and hopes that as her brother-in-law Sir James will
help her.

Dorothea visits Lowick, Casaubon's home. Here she meets Will
Ladislaw, a second cousin of Mr Casaubon though much younger. It is
obvious that neither Will nor Mr Casaubon like one another though
Mr Casaubon supports Will financially.

Before the marriage Mr Brooke gives another dinner party at the
Grange to which he invites all the important people from the town of
Middlemarch. Among those present are the mayor, Mr Vincy, a
manufacturer, his brother-in-law, Mr Bulstrode, a banker, and the
new doctor, Tertius Lydgate, who is to head the new hospital and who
comes from an aristocratic family.

Rosamond and Fred are the daughter and son of Mr Vincy.
Rosamond is beautiful, egocentric, and socially ambitious. Fred is
good-natured but irresponsible. He is in debt and he decides to go with
Rosamond to visit his rich and miserly uncle, Mr Featherstone who is
looked after by Mary Garth whom Fred wants to marry. Lydgate, who
is Mr Featherstone's doctor, arrives when they are there. Rosamond
decides that he would be a perfect husband for her. He is attracted to
Rosamond but is determined not to marry for some years.

Book Two

The medical board of the new hospital meets to appoint a new chaplain. Lydgate prefers Mr Farebrother but because he needs Mr Bulstrode's help he votes for Mr Tyke, the man whom the hypocritical Bulstrode supports.

Meanwhile Dorothea and Casaubon are spending their honeymoon in Rome. Dorothea is beginning to have doubts about Casaubon's research. In Rome she meets Will Ladislaw who confirms her fears and tells her that he is returning to England. Will and Dorothea are drawn towards one another and Mr Casaubon senses this.

Book Three
Fred loses most of the money that he got from his uncle which means he is forced to tell Caleb Garth, the honest but fairly poor father of Mary, that he is unable to pay his debt. Mary tells him that she can never marry a man who has acted as he has.

Fred falls very ill. Mr Wrench, the Vincy's doctor, makes a wrong diagnosis and Fred's condition deteriorates. Lydgate is called in, realises that Fred has typhoid fever, and manages to save him. This makes Lydgate popular with the Vincys but unpopular with the rest of the doctors in Middlemarch.

Dorothea and Casaubon return to England. Casaubon has a heart attack and Lydgate tells Dorothea that he might live another fifteen years but he might also die suddenly.

Because of a certain degree of social pressure and the persuasiveness of Rosamond's tears Lydgate asks her father's permission to marry her. Mr Vincy agrees.

Book Four
Peter Featherstone eventually dies. He surprises all his greedy relatives by leaving his estate to Joshua Rigg and his money to build almshouses for old men.

Dorothea becomes increasingly disillusioned with Casaubon. At the same time the affection between her and Will increases, so much so that Casaubon is convinced that Will is trying to ruin his marriage. Mr Brooke, who has political ambitions, has invited Will to take over the newspaper that Mr Brooke has bought. Casaubon tells Will if he accepts Mr Brooke's offer he will no longer be welcome at Lowick. Will disregards this threat.

Caleb Garth is asked to manage both Sir James Chetlam's estate, Freshitt Hall, and Tipton Grange. He suggests that Fred Vincy might like to become his apprentice instead of becoming a clergyman.

Book Five
Dorothea grows more and more disillusioned with Mr Casaubon's research, so much so that when he asks her to continue his work should he die she at first refuses. She changes her mind the next morning but Mr Casaubon has died. He has left a clause in his will stating that

should Dorothea marry Will Ladislaw she would lose all the property he has left her. Dorothea declares that she has no intention of marrying anyone and that she proposes to devote her time and money to her former plan for workers' cottages. She also offers to support Lydgate and his hospital and on his suggestion she appoints Mr Farebrother rector at Lowick. Mr Farebrother would like to marry Mary Garth but gives up this idea when she tells him that the only person she will marry is Fred.

After a disastrous campaign Mr Brooke retires from politics and dismisses Will. The latter has no knowledge of the clause in the will but he knows that any approach he might make to Dorothea would be looked upon by the others as an attempt to marry her for her money. Meanwhile Joshua Rigg's stepfather, Raffles, begins to blackmail Bulstrode.

Book Six

Dorothea continues to live at Lowick Manor. After several encounters with Will she realises that they love one another but can see no hope of their ever marrying.

She employs Caleb Garth to help her with her plans for the cottages. Fred Vincy has become Caleb's apprentice and Mary indicates that if he makes a success of the job she is willing to marry him.

Lydgate sinks deeper and deeper into debt and Rosamond refuses to help him. She also tells Will of the codicil in Casaubon's will.

We now learn why Raffles is able to blackmail Bulstrode. Raffles knew Bulstrode many years before when the latter worked for Mr Dunkirk, a receiver of stolen goods. Bulstrode knew about Mr Dunkirk's activities but his greed overcame his religious and moral scruples. It was his greed that also led him to cheat Dunkirk's daughter of the fortune that was rightly hers. Raffles reveals to Bulstrode and to Will that this woman was Will's mother. In an attempt to salve his conscience Bulstrode offers Will five hundred pounds a year but Will refuses.

Book Seven

Lydgate is now desperate for money and after several unsuccessful attempts to raise a thousand pounds he is forced to go to Bulstrode and ask him for a loan. Bulstrode refuses and at the same time informs Lydgate that he is giving up his support of the hospital.

The same day Caleb Garth goes to Bulstrode and tells him that he has found Raffles wandering by the roadside very ill and that he has taken him to Stone Court which Bulstrode now owns. Bulstrode asks Lydgate to attend Raffles and fearing what Raffles might reveal when he is delirious offers to lend Lydgate the thousand pounds. Lydgate gives Bulstrode strict instructions that Raffles must not be given alcohol. Whilst Bulstrode does not himself give Raffles alcohol he does not prevent his housekeeper from doing so and Raffles dies. Before he died Raffles had revealed Mr Bulstrode's past to Mr Bambridge, the horse-dealer. Soon the whole town knows, Mr Bulstrode is publicly disgraced and Lydgate comes under the suspicion of having accepted a bribe from the banker.

Book Eight
Dorothea refuses to believe Lydgate guilty. She assures him of her support and offers him a thousand pounds so he can repay Bulstrode. This he does and after paying his creditors he and Rosamond leave Middlemarch. Lydgate gives up his research and becomes a successful doctor in London. He dies when comparatively young and Rosamond marries a rich and much older doctor. Will returns to Middlemarch and after one more misunderstanding he and Dorothea declare their love for one another and decide to marry. They too move to London and Will becomes a successful politician. Eventually they are reconciled with Sir James Chettam who had opposed the marriage, and Dorothea's son inherits Tipton Grange. The Bulstrodes leave Middlemarch but before they do Mr Bulstrode agrees to Fred Vincy becoming manager of Stone Court. This means that he and Mary can marry.

Detailed summaries
BOOK ONE: MISS BROOKE

Chapter 1

We meet Dorothea who is beautiful and rich. She wears plain clothes because, first, she regards fancy clothes and jewels as vulgar and, second, she has Puritanical tendencies and the Puritans frowned upon such things. She has intellectual aspirations and a desire to do great things. She tends to scorn the ordinary things in life and people are a little afraid of her. We also meet her sister Celia who is more practical and ready to act according to the customs and conventions of society. The two sisters are orphans and live with their uncle, Mr Brooke. Celia asks Dorothea if they may share their mother's jewels. Dorothea gives them all to her, keeping only an emerald bracelet and ring because she is attracted by their beauty. Celia is aware of Dorothea's weakness but says nothing to her sister.

Mr Brooke, their uncle, is an amiable man with no fixed opinions, who will always take the easy way out. Though he is kind he is inclined towards meanness.

COMMENTARY: This chapter introduces us to several of the main characters and tells us something about a) the position of women in England at the time, and b) the social hierarchy. By contrasting the two sisters George Eliot brings out clearly their main characteristics and we are immediately made aware of the problems Dorothea is going to have distinguishing between illusion and reality.

NOTES AND GLOSSARY:

Pascal's Pensées: a defence of Christianity against freethinkers by Blaise Pascal (1623–62)

Jeremy Taylor: (1613–67) an Anglican clergyman who wrote *Holy Living* and *Holy Dying*

Mr Peel's late conduct: Sir Robert Peel (1788–1850), Tory leader who changed his mind about Catholic emancipation. See 'Religion and the Catholic question' in Part 3

judicious Hooker: Richard Hooker (1553–1600), Bishop of Exeter and author of *Of the Laws of Ecclesiastical Polity*. He made an unfortunate marriage

Henrietta-Maria: (1605–69) wife to King Charles I of England

Chapter 2

Sir James Chettam and the Reverend Edward Casaubon are dining at Mr Brooke's house. Sir James, a simple, kind man, aware of his own limitations, wishes to marry Dorothea. He realises that she is intelligent, but, instead of being put off by this, he is pleased about it, because she can help him to solve his problems. He is not worried because he adheres to the traditional opinion that female intellect, no matter how high it is, is of a different and inferior quality to the male.

Dorothea scorns Sir James though she considers whether he would be a suitable husband for Celia. She is infatuated by the Reverend Casaubon who she believes must be very wise as well as being very holy. She regards him with awe and senses that he has intellectual aspirations the same as her own. Sir James regards Casaubon as 'a dried bookworm' nearly fifty years of age.

COMMENTARY: The epigraph from the novel *Don Quixote* (1605) by the Spanish author Miguel de Cervantes (1547–1616) draws our attention to the point George Eliot is trying to make about illusion and reality. And as in Chapter 1 she illustrates her point by contrasting the reaction of the two sisters to the Reverend Casaubon. The practical Celia sees him as he is, 'very ugly'. Dorothea on the other hand thinks 'he is one of the most distinguished-looking men' she has ever seen.

Dorothea is revealed as being not only naïve but also a little smug in her righteousness, 'too religious for family comfort', thinks Celia. The position of women is also discussed in this chapter.

NOTES AND GLOSSARY:

Locke:	John Locke (1632–1704), philosopher
Adam Smith:	(1723–90) economist, author of *The Wealth of Nations*
Southey:	Robert Southey (1774–1843), poet and essayist
the Waldenses:	a religious sect in France persecuted as heretics
Wilberforce:	William Wilberforce (1759–1833), a philanthropist and politician who led the campaign to abolish slavery
cochon de lait:	(*French*) sucking-pig
Mawworm:	a sanctimonious hypocrite in Isaac Bickerstaff's play *The Hypocrite* (1769)

Chapter 3

Mr Casaubon explains to Dorothea what his great work is about. He is attempting to show 'all the mythical systems or erratic mythical fragments in the world were corruptions of a tradition originally revealed'. This makes Dorothea admire him even more and regard him as 'a modern Augustine who united the glories of doctor and saint'. Mr Casaubon tells her that he is lonely and this leads her to hope that he will marry her. Only one thing disappoints her about Mr Casaubon and that is that he shows no interest in the cottages she hopes to build for the poor workers. Sir James Chettam, however, is interested in her plans, both because he is kind and also because he hopes to win her favour in this way. Dorothea is pleased because she believes Sir James will marry Celia and then as her brother-in-law will carry out her scheme.

COMMENTARY: George Eliot enters directly into this chapter (a technique known as authorial intrusion) and takes up the Saint Theresa theme of the Prelude. In the previous chapters she has shown Dorothea to be naïve, priggish and smug. But if she is all of these things she also possesses positive qualities and George Eliot asks us to appreciate these and to understand Dorothea, 'the offspring of a certain spiritual grandeur ill-matched with the meanness of opportunity' and with the times.

NOTES AND GLOSSARY:

Bossuet:	Jacques Bénigne Bossuet (1627–1704), a famous French preacher in the seventeenth century
Augustine:	St Augustine (AD354–430), one of the Church fathers
Rhamnus:	a small coastal town close to Athens, with the remains of an ancient temple and an ancient fortress

custos rotulorum: (*Latin*) the keeper of the local records—hardly a task for Mr Brooke

Feejeean: belonging to the island of Fiji. George Eliot is satirising the current fashion in hair styles. She always wore her hair in a very plain style

Female Scripture Characters: a well-known book by Mrs F. E. King, published in 1813

Loudon's book: *A Manual of Cottage Gardening, Husbandry and Architecture* (1830) by J. C. Loudon (1783–1843)

Oberlin: J. F. Oberlin (1770–1826), a French Protestant reformer and philanthropist

Chapter 4

Celia tells Dorothea that it is Dorothea, and not herself, that Sir James wishes to marry. Dorothea is angry that he should think she would even consider marrying him. Mr Brooke returns home and tells Dorothea that Mr Casaubon has asked for her hand in marriage. Mr Brooke finds Sir James a more suitable partner but says that if Dorothea wishes to marry Mr Casaubon (who might become a bishop) he has no objection to the marriage. Dorothea tells her uncle that she will be happy to accept Mr Casaubon.

COMMENTARY: Dorothea believes that ·in marrying Mr Casaubon and 'getting away from Tipton and Freshitt' she is getting away from 'her own sad liability to tread in the wrong places on her way to the New Jerusalem'. This is a case of dramatic irony. The author has already revealed enough for us to know that Dorothea is suffering from an illusion and that her escape will in fact lead to a further enslavement.

NOTES AND GLOSSARY:

nullifidian: a sceptic

Romilly: Sir Samuel Romilly (1757–1818), politician, pioneer of law reform, favoured Catholic emancipation and the abolition of slavery. He committed suicide

if Peel stays in: Peel resigned when the Wellington government fell in November 1830

Chapter 5

Mr Casaubon writes Dorothea a letter proposing marriage. He tells her that he has a special need and that he considers that she is fit to supply this need. Dorothea replies, accepting his offer and telling him that she will be honoured to be his wife. Celia is horrified when Dorothea informs her that she is going to marry Mr Casaubon. That evening Mr Casaubon comes to dinner. He and Dorothea discuss their future and decide that the wedding should take place in six weeks' time.

COMMENTARY: Celia, the touchstone of reality, has already seen Mr Casaubon for what in truth he is. He now betrays himself through his letter of proposal in which he shows himself to be conceited and more in need of a nurse than a wife. Dorothea fails to see through this. George Eliot, however, does not condemn her. She reveals a sympathy and understanding of Dorothea, and of 'a mind struggling towards an ideal life'. If Dorothea is naïve she is also sincere and George Eliot forgives her, asking us to consider 'what believer sees a disturbing omission or infelicity'.

The author has, however, already sounded the warning and we might say that the 'theme of disenchantment' found so frequently in George Eliot's novels has been introduced. From now on we are going to witness Dorothea's growing disillusionment and her final coming to terms with reality.

Chapter 6

Mrs Cadwallader, wife of the Rector, calls on Mr Brooke. She too is horrified to hear that Dorothea is to marry Mr Casaubon, the more so as she had tried to arrange a marriage between Dorothea and Sir James Chettam. She is also a little worried that Mr Brooke may stand as a liberal candidate in the next elections. She hurries to break the news to Sir James and consoles him by saying that he has had a lucky miss and would be much better off marrying Celia. Sir James is disappointed, but not for long, and eventually rides to Mr Brooke's house with the intention of paying more attention to Celia.

COMMENTARY: This chapter introduces us to Mrs Cadwallader, one of the minor characters who add humour to the novel. She has a sharp tongue but often a witty one, as her remark 'One can't eat fowls of a bad character at a high price' reveals. Mrs Cadwallader is a snob; she is high-born and has married beneath her but, for her, poverty is not a crime, the crime is to be low-born. This means she has a particular loathing for the *nouveaux riches*, especially for the inhabitants of the town who have made their money through business. She upholds the traditional values, and for this reason is upset that Mr Brooke may join the Whig party. Though she is a busybody who tries to arrange and rule other people's lives (Mr Brooke is terrified of her) she is not presented as a malicious character.

The last sentence in this chapter again points to the fact that Sir James Chettam is a kind man.

NOTES AND GLOSSARY:

Thirty-nine Articles: essential beliefs of the Church of England, to be found in the Anglican *Book of Common Prayer*

***varium et mutabile semper*:** (*Latin*) varied and always changing

poor Stoddart: this may refer to Sir John Stoddart (1773-1856)

the Moravian Brethren: the Moravian church inspired by John Hus was founded in the fifteenth century in Bohemia. It was particularly famous for its missionary zeal and its work in education

Seven Sages: the wise men of ancient Greece

Sappho's apple: Sappho was the best-known poetess of ancient times. In one of her poems she compares a young bride to an unplucked apple

Chapter 7

Because of his forthcoming marriage Mr Casaubon spends a good deal of time at the Grange. He is a little irritated by this as it takes him away from his work. He also wonders why he cannot be more enthusiastic about being in love. Dorothea persuades him to teach her Greek so she can help him with his work. Mr Brooke cannot understand how Dorothea could love Casaubon, but he accepts the fact and consoles himself with the thought that Casaubon is likely to become a bishop.

COMMENTARY: This chapter shows the lack of passion and love in the Dorothea/Casaubon relationship: Casaubon is marrying Dorothea not because he loves her but because he wants 'female tendance for his declining years'. Dorothea is marrying Casaubon because she believes he will guide her towards the intellectual heights to which she aspires. In her comments on the situation the author reveals her understanding and tolerance of the foibles of human nature; 'it is', she says 'a narrow mind which cannot look at a subject from various points of view'.

Chapter 8

Sir James is very concerned about Dorothea marrying Mr Casaubon, whom he regards as a cold man without a heart. He asks the rector, Mr Cadwallader, to go to Mr Brooke and persaude him at least to postpone the marriage until Dorothea is of age. Mr Cadwallader, who looks for the good and not the bad in his fellow men, refuses to do so because, first, he says there is nothing wrong with Mr Casaubon, and, second, he knows he could not persuade Mr Brooke.

Even though Dorothea will not marry him Sir James continues with his plan to build the cottages and in his further conversations with Dorothea on the subject a relaxed friendship grows between them.

COMMENTARY: In this chapter we can admire George Eliot's ability to present the essentials of a man's character with small deft touches. The fact that Mr Cadwallader keeps his fishing-tackle in his study tells us much about this good-hearted, down-to-earth man, who has the ability to see 'the joke of any satire against himself'. We can see how useful this ability must be to a man married to Mrs Cadwallader.

NOTES AND GLOSSARY:

Xisuthrus: Xisuthrus was the equivalent of Noah in Babylonian mythology

Chapter 9

Dorothea, Celia and Mr Brooke visit Mr Casaubon's house so that Dorothea can suggest any necessary changes. Dorothea refuses to make any changes declaring that it is perfect as it is. They meet Mr Tucker, the curate, who tells them that the villagers are well cared for. Dorothea is a little sad about this, as she had hoped to perform good deeds among the poor. They also meet Will Ladislaw, Mr Casaubon's young cousin. Will is undecided as to what he will do and Mr Casaubon has agreed to finance him so that he can spend several more years in Europe.

COMMENTARY: The world outside the narrow sphere of Dorothea and Celia had already been introduced through the references to Mr Brooke's political inclinations and Mrs Cadwallader's comments about the *nouveaux riches* in the towns. Mrs Cadwallader believes in the superiority of the country over the town with all that this implies, for in the country the traditional beliefs, both religious and cultural, are still upheld and the social hierarchy still maintained. We find the same division between the country and the town in another novel by George Eliot, *Silas Marner* (1861).

NOTES AND GLOSSARY:

Renaissance-Corregiosities: a mocking reference to Antonio da Corregio (1494-1534), painter, particularly of Madonna and Child pictures

Æolian harp: a musical instrument

Bruce or a Mungo Park: James Bruce (1730-94) and Mungo Park (1771-1806) were both African explorers

Chapter 10

Will Ladislaw leaves once again for the continent. Mr Casaubon is a little upset that he is not more excited about his approaching marriage. He and Dorothea are going to Rome for their honeymoon because

Mr Casaubon wants to examine some manuscripts at the Vatican. Mr Brooke gives a pre-marriage dinner party for Dorothea to which he invites the local landed gentry and the important citizens of the neighbouring town of Middlemarch. These include Mr Lydgate, a doctor with a reputation for advanced ideas about medicine.

COMMENTARY: This is a transitional chapter which links the world of Tipton Grange and that of Middlemarch. The latter, which had been only briefly mentioned before, is now treated in more detail and we are introduced to the people who inhabit it and who will play an important role in the story. The chapter emphasises the differences between the town and the country, the different kinds of people who inhabit each and the prejudices each group holds about the other.

To counteract these prejudices George Eliot, using a narrative technique common to her work, that of authorial intrusion, breaks into the story and warns the reader about making hasty judgements.

The theme of disenchantment, mentioned earlier, is taken one step further when Dorothea is for the first time annoyed with Mr Casaubon.

NOTES AND GLOSSARY:

De Quincey: Thomas De Quincey (1785-1859), English essayist who wrote *Confessions of an English Opium Eater* (1821)

an immortal physicist: probably refers to Thomas Young (1773-1829), physicist and Egyptologist

Stoics and Alexandrians: refers to Greek schools of philosophy

Broussais: Francois Broussais (1772-1838), famous French surgeon and physician

---

Chapter 11

Lydgate decides that Dorothea is not his style of woman. The woman he is fascinated by is Rosamond Vincy, the daughter of the mayor of Middlemarch, a wealthy manufacturer, but he does not contemplate marriage yet as he is both poor and ambitious and there are many things he plans to do before he settles down.

The morning after the party we find Rosamond Vincy and her mother at home. Rosamond has social ambitions and wishes her father had not made his wealth through business. She has decided not to marry any young man from Middlemarch. On this particular morning she is irritated by her brother Fred who insists on getting up late unless he is going hunting. Rosamond talks Fred into letting her come riding with him to Stone Court which is owned by her wealthy and ailing uncle, Mr Featherstone. He is looked after by Mary Garth, who is his niece and whose family is poor.

COMMENTARY: This chapter emphasises two things: (1) the way one life will affect another in spite of our efforts to the contrary: 'Destiny stands by sarcastic with our *dramatis personae* folded in her hand'; (2) that this is a period of social change and mobility in which 'Municipal town and rural parish gradually made fresh threads of connection—gradually, as the old stocking gave way to the savings-bank'.

NOTES AND GLOSSARY:

the solar guinea:	a gold coin which ceased to be minted after 1813. It was replaced by the sovereign
Herodotus:	Greek historian (*c.*480–*c.*425BC)
Ar hyd y nos:	Welsh song, 'All through the night'

Chapter 12

Next morning Fred and Rosamond ride over to visit their uncle, Mr Featherstone. He already has a visitor, his sister, Mrs Waule, who urges him to leave his money to her children and not to Fred Vincy who, she says, is gambling too much. She also reports that Fred proposes to pay his debts by getting a mortgage on his uncle's property which he hopes to inherit.

When Fred and Rosamond arrive Mr Featherstone rudely dismisses his sister and tells Rosamond to go and talk to Mary as he wishes to speak to Fred. He then tells Fred what Mrs Waule has said and asks him if it is true. Fred denies it, but Mr Featherstone says he will only believe him if he brings him a note from his other uncle, Mr Bulstrode, the banker, saying it is not true.

Meanwhile Rosamond talks to Mary and discovers that the latter is not interested in Mr Lydgate but in Fred. This pleases Rosamond as she is interested in Lydgate herself. At this moment Lydgate calls to visit his patient, Mr Featherstone. It is the first direct confrontation between Rosamond and Lydgate and they are immediately attracted to one another.

On the ride home Rosamond thinks what an excellent husband Mr Lydgate would make and Fred reluctantly decides to ask his father to help him get the letter from Mr Bulstrode as he cannot afford to displease his uncle.

COMMENTARY: Again by comparing and contrasting characters George Eliot brings out their virtues and vices. Rosamond and Lydgate, like Dorothea and Mr Casaubon, are interested in one another for selfish reasons. On the other hand Fred's love for Mary is genuine and Mary's honesty and generosity contrast sharply with Rosamond's hypocrisy and selfishness. Mr Featherstone's only interest is in money and there is an indication that money will play a significant role in the lives of some of the characters.

This chapter ends Book One and it is useful to see what has been established so far: (1) a series of interlocking relationships which will join both country and town; (2) a dichotomy between the town and the country with an indication that there will be an increasing influence of one on the other and that the values of the town will eventually supersede those of the country; (3) the motivation behind most people's interests in one another is not love but self-interest.

NOTES AND GLOSSARY:

an articled pupil: similar to an apprentice. In exchange for an education she would do some teaching

Josephus, Culpepper . . . *Magazine*: Flavius Josephus (AD37-100), a Jewish historian; Sir Thomas Culpepper, a seventeenth-century writer on usury, and Friedrich Klopstock (1724-1802), the German poet who wrote the religious epic *Der Messias* (1773). *The Gentleman's Magazine* was a conservative periodical founded in 1731

***il y en a pour tous les goûts*:** (*French*) there is something for all tastes

old Overreach: Sir Giles Overreach is the cruel, usurous villain of Philip Massinger's play *A New Way to Pay Old Debts* (1633)

BOOK TWO: OLD AND YOUNG

Chapter 13

Mr Vincy agrees to speak to Mr Bulstrode. When he calls at the banker's office he finds Mr Lydgate there. Mr Lydgate and Mr Bulstrode are discussing the new fever hospital. Mr Bulstrode soon makes it clear that he is more interested in the patients' spiritual well-being than in their physical health and that he will support Mr Lydgate if the latter will support Mr Bulstrode's candidate for the hospital chaplaincy. Mr Lydgate replies in an honest fashion, saying that he is interested in the patients' physical health and not their spiritual needs. An argument is about to take place when Mr Vincy arrives and Mr Lydgate leaves.

Mr Vincy tells Mr Bulstrode why he has come and Mr Bulstrode promptly tells him that he is unwilling to write the letter and starts moralising, telling Vincy that he has spoilt Fred. Eventually Vincy loses his patience and tells Bulstrode that he is a hypocrite. Bulstrode is displeased. However, he agrees to talk the matter over with his wife, Vincy's sister, because he maintains he does not wish to split the family.

Chapter 14

Mr Bulstrode writes the letter and the next morning Fred delivers it to his uncle. Mr Featherstone takes malicious pleasure in humiliating Fred but Fred endeavours to hide his true feelings because he wants the money. Eventually his uncle gives him a hundred pounds which is much less than Fred had hoped for.

Fred goes upstairs to talk to Mary and tries to get her to promise to marry him. Mary refuses to do so saying that she would not marry anyone who lived such an idle life as Fred does. Mr Lydgate comes to visit Mr Featherstone and Fred rides home, still not without hope that Mary will marry him. He gives his mother eighty pounds to keep towards his debt of one hundred and sixty pounds and keeps twenty pounds for himself.

COMMENTARY (Chapters 13-14): 'No man is an island' could be the epigraph (a quotation at the beginning of a chapter, or of a book) to these two chapters, indeed to the whole book, for George Eliot is constantly pointing out how each one of us is in some way dependent on others. The two chapters show two reactions to this situation. Lydgate's honesty with Bulstrode is contrasted with Fred's lack of integrity with his uncle. Lydgate's genuine concern for humanity is also contrasted with Bulstrode's pious moral hypocrisy and the sharp difference between the latter's statements and his non-charitable actions. Compare the epigraph to Chapter 13:

> 1ST GENT: How class your man?—as better than the most,
>   Or, seeming better, worse beneath that cloak?

Mary's honesty and common sense are further stressed.

NOTES AND GLOSSARY:

Brenda Troil: Brenda and Minna Troil, Merton and Cleveland are all characters in Sir Walter Scott's *The Pirate* (1822)

Waverley and Flora MacIvor: characters in Scott's *Waverley* (1814)

Olivia and Sophia Primrose: characters in Oliver Goldsmith's *The Vicar of Wakefield* (1766)

Corinne: the heroine in a novel of the same name (1807) by Madame de Staël

Chapter 15

George Eliot spends some time at the beginning of this chapter on the scientific aspects of medicine. This is done to make us realise that

Lydgate is not an ordinary run-of-the-mill doctor. We are then given a retrospective picture of Lydgate, describing his decision to become a doctor. He chose the medical profession because he believed it presented 'the most perfect interchange between science and art'. He was particularly interested in medical reform and he believed he could help people. As a young doctor living in Paris he had fallen in love with an actress who had accidentally, he believed, stabbed her husband during a performance. He proposed to her, and was horrified when she told him the stabbing was not an accident. Lydgate resolved that from then on 'he would take a strictly scientific view of woman'.

COMMENTARY: This chapter reveals that Lydgate has a genuine concern for medicine and for its reform and that he can make a positive contribution to medical science. This is important to remember later on when both Bulstrode and Rosamond thwart his efforts in research. It also shows why he has certain failings concerning women. The author reveals that Lydgate, like all men, has weaknesses but is essentially a good man.

NOTES AND GLOSSARY:

Fielding: Henry Fielding (1707-54), novelist. The reference here is to his novel *Tom Jones* (1749)

Rasselas: *Rasselas* (1759) by Samuel Johnson

Gulliver: *Gulliver's Travels* (1762) by Jonathan Swift

Bailey's Dictionary: a forerunner to Dr Johnson's *Dictionary*

London, Edinburgh, and Paris: Lydgate's attendance at these universities indicates he had the best possible medical education

Jenner: Edward Jenner (1749-1823), discoverer of vaccination

graduates of Oxford and Cambridge: this is ironical. At a time when the standards of medical education were very bad those at Oxford and Cambridge were particularly so. Here the education of a physician was primarily classical and only secondarily medical. What is more, little attempt was made to enforce standards and many pretended to degrees they did not have

Herschel: Sir William Herschel (1738-1822), astronomer and discoverer of Uranus

a recent legal decision: the Apothecaries Act of 1815 insisted on qualifications for dispensing chemists. This passage refers to one of the many legal cases which occurred as a result of this act (possibly Allison *v.* Haydon, 1828)

Bichat: François Bichat (1771-1802), a pioneer in

anatomical pathology. This branch of medicine was much more advanced in France because it required post-mortem examination and there was less prejudice against this in France than in England

the Saint Simonians: followers of Comte de Saint-Simon (1760-1825), the French philosopher, socialist and supporter of women's rights

Porte Saint Martin: the best-known of the French melodrama theatres

Chapter 16

Lydgate is attending a party at the Vincys' and the question of who should be the hospital chaplain is discussed. Lydgate expresses the opinion that the post should go to the best-qualified man even though he may not necessarily be the most agreeable.

Rosamond and Lydgate discuss music and when she sings and plays he becomes even more fascinated by her. Also attending the dinner party is Farebrother who is one of the candidates for the hospital chaplaincy, a pleasant man who obviously enjoys playing whist.

Lydgate returns home and soon forgets Rosamond as he becomes absorbed in his work and his ambition to make great discoveries and so improve the lot of mankind. He intends to marry and when he does so it will be to a girl like Rosamond. But this will not be for at least five years. First he must make his reputation and some money.

Rosamond on the other hand looks upon Lydgate as an immediate and ideal marriage partner, much superior to the other suitors from Middlemarch. One thing that especially attracts her to him is his upper-class birth. She has social ambitions and believes that if she marries Lydgate she will move nearer to the social status of the Miss Brookes.

COMMENTARY: The author indicates that Bulstrode does good deeds not for the love of mankind but in order to gain mastery over people. His pleasure is not in food and drink but a 'vampire's feast in the sense of mastery'. Notice the different motivations of Lydgate and Rosamond for their interest in one another and the later effect of this on their lives.

One other contrast is between the joy and richness of life in the Vincy home with the subtle hint that no such enjoyment of life exists in Bulstrode's house.

NOTES AND GLOSSARY:

Wakley: Thomas Wakley (1765-1862), physician and founder of the medical journal *The Lancet* (1823). He was a radical reformer, one of whose demands

was that the coroner should have medical and not
legal qualifications

prick-eared: means 'priggish', and is derived from the close-
cropped hair style of the Roundheads

the plucked Fred: means that Fred failed his examinations

like a Niobe before her troubles: Niobe, who had seven sons and seven
daughters, had shown contempt for Leto who only
had twins. But these twins were the gods Apollo
and Artemis and they destroyed every one of
Niobe's children

Louis: Pierre Louis (1787-1872), a French physician
famous for his work on typhoid fever

'Lalla Rookh': a popular poem (1817) by the poet and song-writer
Thomas Moore (1779-1852)

Chapter 17

Lydgate visits Mr Farebrother and meets the latter's mother, aunt and
sister. Farebrother is anxious to show Lydgate his insect collection. It
becomes clear that he knows that he would have been a better
naturalist than a clergyman but it is too late to change. Farebrother
warns Lydgate that if he votes for him he will offend Bulstrode and that
he should be careful of doing this. He also tells Lydgate that if he votes
for Mr Tyke, Bulstrode's candidate, it will have no effect on their
relationship. However, he admits that he would regret losing the forty
pounds which the post would bring him.

COMMENTARY: 'Why, Camden!' said Miss Winifred, 'Griffin and his
wife told me only to-day, that Mr Tyke said they should have no more
coals if they came to hear you preach.' This is a direct reference back to
the previous chapter and emphasises the way Bulstrode uses power
and manipulates people for his own ends. At this stage Lydgate naively
believes that each man can remain independent of others; through lack
of experience he has no understanding of the true nature of the
situation.

NOTES AND GLOSSARY:

anencephalous: lacking the brain

***Aphis Brassicae*:** a garden pest that feeds on cabbages

Philomicron: a *nom-de-plume* meaning 'lover of the small'

Pythagorean community: a Utopia for those who practise socialism.
There are a number of references in the novel to
Utopian communities. Trawley was possibly
influenced by Saint-Simon. His eventual fate
parallels that of Lydgate

Robert Brown:	a famous botanist (1773-1853). The work referred to appeared in the *Edinburgh New Philosophical Journal,* 1828

Chapter 18

Lydgate's friendship with Farebrother deepens, though he worries a little about the fact that the clergyman likes to play cards and billiards for money. He knows also that if he votes for Tyke he will gain Bulstrode's favour and this matters if there is to be money for his work. There is a meeting and the casting vote is left to Lydgate, who votes for Tyke. Lydgate is conscious of the fact that his motive for voting for Tyke was a selfish one and if there had been no pressure on him he would have voted for Farebrother. Farebrother, however, remains his friend.

COMMENTARY: Lydgate is forced for the first time to admit that forces other than moral ones influence one's actions. In this particular instance the opportunist wins over the moralist.

NOTES AND GLOSSARY:

Prodicus:	a Sophist and contemporary of Socrates (?470-399BC), the Athenian philosopher. He wrote the famous myth, 'The Choice of Hercules'

Chapter 19

The story shifts to Rome and the next scene takes place in the Vatican where a young German artist, Adolf Naumann, sees a woman whose beauty he believes puts the statues to shame. He draws his friend Will Ladislaw's attention to her and Will realises it is Dorothea. Naumann wishes to paint her but for some reason Will is opposed to this, and says Dorothea would not wish to be painted.

NOTES AND GLOSSARY:

the most brilliant English critic of the day:	a reference to William Hazlitt (1778-1830)
German artists:	early in the nineteenth century a group of German artists with religious leanings settled in Rome. They were known as the Nazarenes
***Geistlicher*:**	(*German*) a clergyman
Antigone:	in Greek myth the daughter of Oedipus, and the Greek ideal of devotion to a parent. This indicates that Naumann regards Casaubon as Dorothea's father and not as her husband

Chapter 20

Two hours later Dorothea is at home in her room sobbing, though for
what exact reason she is not quite certain. She is disillusioned with
Casaubon and has begun to realise that he is not the great scholar she
took him to be. Casaubon too is worried; he asks himself whether
'instead of getting a soft fence against the cold, shadowy, unapplausive
audience of his life, [he had] only given it a more substantial presence?'
He also depresses Dorothea by rejecting any affection she may show
towards him. That morning at breakfast they had quarrelled for the
first time and Dorothea was brooding over that quarrel and her future
when Naumann first saw her.

NOTES AND GLOSSARY:
Cabeiri: a group of Samothracian fertility gods

Chapter 21

Will visits Dorothea and observes that she has been crying. He realises
that his first judgement of her was wrong and is impressed by her. They
discuss art and Will tells her that he has decided not to become an artist.
The discussion then turns to Casaubon and Will points out that he is
wasting his time because the work he is doing has already been done by
German scholars. Dorothea is distressed to hear this. Casaubon returns
home weary and somewhat irritated by Will's presence. Will senses this
and leaves. Dorothea apologises to Casaubon for her behaviour that
morning, an apology that Casaubon takes for granted.

NOTES AND GLOSSARY:
If Mr Casaubon read German: at this time German scholarship led the
world in historical criticism of the Bible.
Casaubon's ignorance of German points out how
much out of touch he is with contemporary
scholarship

COMMENTARY (Chapters 19-21): These chapters reveal the growing
awareness on the part of both Casaubon and Dorothea that they have
made a mistake. Will, who is sharply contrasted with Casaubon, points
out that Casaubon's research is not nearly so advanced as he thinks and
indeed it has been done already by the German philosophers. This
reflects George Eliot's special interest in the subject as does Will's and
Naumann's discussion about poetry and art.

Through the flashback technique (a transition to an earlier scene or
event) George Eliot is able to reveal to us things about the characters
that they are not aware of and so prepare us for events to come.

Chapter 22

Will comes to dinner the next day and goes out of his way to be agreeable. He tells Dorothea and Casaubon that they must not leave Rome before visiting some of the studios and offers to take them the next day. After visiting several he takes them to Naumann's studio. Naumann asks Casaubon if he minds sitting for him as he has just the right head for the picture of Thomas Aquinas that he is painting. Casaubon is flattered and agrees to pose. He is unaware that this is only an excuse so that Naumann may also paint Dorothea, which he does. Casaubon buys his own picture but not Dorothea's.

By now Will is completely infatuated with Dorothea and contrives to visit her the next day when she is alone. They discuss art and poetry and once more Casaubon's work is mentioned.

COMMENTARY: Like Chapter 10, this is a transitional chapter in which the scene is set for a return to England. The stay in Rome has not only brought about 'a tottering faith' especially for Dorothea, but it has also established a new set of relationships which will create future conflicts.

NOTES AND GLOSSARY:

Middleton:	Conyers Middleton (1683-1750), a theological controversialist. Another indication of how out of date Mr Casaubon is
Laocoon:	a famous sculpture in Florence by Michelangelo Buonarotti (1475-1564). In Greek mythology Laocoon was a priest of the god Apollo at Troy who warned the Trojans against the wooden horse left by the Greeks (by means of which they took the city). He was killed with his two sons by two sea serpents
Thorwaldsen:	Bertel Thorvaldsen (1770-1844), a Danish sculptor who lived in Rome
***pfuscherei*:**	(*colloquial German*) a mess
Minotaurs:	the Minotaur was a monster in classical mythology who had the head of a bull and a human body. He was killed by Theseus
Paracelsus:	(1493-1541) a famous Swiss physician
Bryant:	Jacob Bryant (1715-1804), author of *An Analysis of Ancient Mythology*
Chus and Mizraim:	two sons of Ham, son of Noah. Said to be the ancestors of a number of tribes in ancient Egypt. See the Bible, Genesis 10

BOOK THREE: WAITING FOR DEATH

Chapter 23

The scene returns to England and to Fred Vincy who is worried about the money he owes the horse-dealer, Mr Bambridge. Caleb Garth, the father of Mary, had signed the bill for it, and Fred hopes to repay the money without involving Caleb. He tries first of all to win at billiards with the twenty pounds he had kept but he soon loses this. He then goes to a nearby horse-fair where he trades his horse plus thirty pounds for a dappled grey horse called Diamond. Fred is pleased with his deal because he knows that Lord Medlicote wants such a horse and he hopes to sell Diamond to him for eighty pounds.

NOTES AND GLOSSARY:

Lindley Murray and Mangnall's *Questions:* two very popular textbooks, *English Grammar* (1795) by Lindley Murray and *Miscellaneous Questions* (1800) by Mrs R. Mangnall

'cute jockies: horse-dealers; the implication is that they are swindlers as well

blacklegs: horse-racing swindlers

sawyers: workers in a timber yard

Chapter 24

Fred soon discovers that he has made a bad bargain, for Diamond turns out to be a vicious horse who in lashing out manages to lame himself. This means that Fred now has only fifty pounds and there is nothing else he can do but to go to Caleb Garth and tell him that he is unable to pay. Caleb and his wife Susan are very upset, for they have little money themselves and it means that the money Sarah had saved for her own son's education will have to be used to pay Fred's debt. They will also have to borrow some money from Mary. For the first time in his life Fred feels genuine remorse and he rides off to visit Mary.

COMMENTARY (Chapters 23-4): Chapter 23 touches again on Fred's blind (and we know) foolish reliance on chance whilst at the same time making it clear that even though he might be foolish he is not unkind.

In Chapter 24 we meet the Garth family and are shown that people can be happy even if they do not have a lot of money. Garth 'could not manage finance' although 'he knew values well'. Their happiness, honesty and integrity are in direct contrast to some other families in the book; for example, the Bulstrodes, even the Vincys.

Chapter 25

Fred rides to Stone Court and tells Mary what has happened. At first she despises him but when she sees how completely dejected he is she relents a little. That evening her father comes to borrow money from her and to warn her against marrying Fred. Mary tells him that he need not worry for she would never marry anyone 'who has no manly independence, and who goes on loitering away his time on the chance that others will provide for him'.

Chapter 26

The next day Fred, who had been feeling ill, feels much worse and the doctor is sent for. Mr Wrench says it is not serious and prescribes certain drugs and leaves. Fred, however, feels even worse the next day, Wrench is not available and Mrs Vincy, seeing Lydgate passing, calls him in. Lydgate examines Fred and realises he is seriously ill, with typhoid fever. Both Mr and Mrs Vincy are angry with Wrench for not diagnosing the disease immediately. Lydgate tries to be diplomatic but Wrench thinks his action unethical and regards him as an outsider and a quack. The result is that Lydgate becomes the Vincys' doctor.

COMMENTARY Chapter 25-6): Again Lydgate is forced to realise that 'no man is an island'. In doing his duty and acting according to his conscience he has once more alienated certain members of the community. This is to have important consequences later on.

Chapter 27

On account of Fred's illness Lydgate visits the Vincy house every day and this means that he and Rosamond see a great deal of one another. Lydgate, because of lack of money and also because of his interest in medical research, has no intention of marrying for some years but he sees no harm in flirting with Rosamond. Rosamond, on the other hand, takes this as an indication that he is anxious to marry her and she determines that he should do so. The author hints that the victory will be Rosamond's. Several of Rosamond's suitors are jealous of Lydgate and this means he creates more enemies.

Fred recovers slowly and is upset that he has not heard from Mary Garth. Lydgate is summoned to Lowick Manor.

NOTES AND GLOSSARY:

the last *Keepsake*: the latest issue of *The Keepsake*, a fashionable and expensive annual publication

Lady Blessington: the Countess of Blessington (1789-1849) also edited *The Keepsake* and wrote novels about aristocratic society

L.E.L.: the pen-name used by Letitia Elizabeth Landon who wrote poems and fashionable novels

Chapter 28

The scene has shifted to Lowick Manor where Dorothea and Casaubon have returned from their honeymoon. Mr Brooke and Celia come to visit them and Mr Brooke remarks on the fact that Casaubon looks pale. Celia informs Dorothea that she is to be married to Sir James Chettam.

COMMENTARY: This chapter stresses Dorothea's growing disillusionment with her marriage and with the 'dream which the dreamer begins to suspect'. She feels a kinship between herself and Will's grandmother who had made an unfortunate marriage. Dorothea now asks herself the question, 'Was it only her friends who thought her marriage unfortunate?' In a manner very typical of her, George Eliot parallels Dorothea's situation with the landscape and the house. The narrowed landscape, the shrunken furniture, the never-read books, the ghostly stag in the pale fantastic world of the tapestry tell us that Dorothea is becoming aware of the true nature of her situation and beginning to realise that instead of gaining her freedom in marriage she has become trapped in 'a still white enclosure'. The images also function as symbols of the abortive and pretentious nature of Casaubon's studies, the narrowness of his world and the dried-up nature of the man. The death-like aspect of the images reflects the relationship between Dorothea and Casaubon, and also prepares us for Casaubon's illness. In yet another set of comparisons George Eliot contrasts Mr Brooke with Casaubon. Mr Brooke warns Casaubon about working too hard. We, the readers, are aware of certain facts. The tragedy for both Casaubon and Dorothea is that they too are being forced to acknowledge them.

Chapter 29

Several weeks have elapsed and Mr Casaubon is sitting in his study writing a small pamphlet. Dorothea joins him and is immediately aware that he is displeased. Casaubon hands Dorothea a letter from Will Ladislaw which was enclosed in a letter he, Casaubon, had received from Will. Before Dorothea has a chance to read her letter Casaubon informs her that Will has asked to stay with them and he,

Casaubon, refuses to have him. This makes Dorothea very angry and she leaves the room without reading the letters. A short while afterwards whilst she is working she hears a noise from her husband's study. She goes to him and discovers that he has collapsed. Just at this moment Celia and Sir James call on a visit and the latter suggests that they send for Dr Lydgate, and Casaubon agrees. This is the summons that was mentioned at the end of Chapter 27.

COMMENTARY: This chapter in some ways parallels the previous one, for if in Chapter 28 George Eliot showed sympathy for and understanding of Dorothea's situation, in Chapter 29 she shows equal sympathy and understanding for Mr Casaubon. She presents him as a somewhat pitiful figure, anxious to achieve great things, yet aware that he will never succeed, like a bird 'thinking of its wings and never flying'. Casaubon is also disillusioned with his marriage. He had married Dorothea hoping for a quiet, docile companion who could also function as his secretary. Instead he finds a person who makes intellectual demands on him that he is unable to fulfil. His marriage can be added to his long list of failures of which he is aware but which he is unable to acknowledge.

NOTES AND GLOSSARY:
Parergon: a work of secondary importance
Brasenose: Brasenose College, Oxford University
the big mask and the speaking-trumpet: these were devices used by actors on the ancient Greek stage to give a larger-than-life dignity to their appearance and to magnify their voices
Warburton: Bishop William Warburton (1698–1779), bishop and critic who was involved in theological controversies. He published an edition of Shakespeare's works

Chapter 30

Lydgate examines Mr Casaubon and reaches the conclusion that he has had a heart attack. He tells Dorothea that he could live for another fifteen years but that he must not work so hard. Dorothea has completely forgotten her anger and her only concern now is to look after Mr Casaubon. She wants to prevent Will Ladislaw from coming to Lowick Manor and she asks her uncle to write to him. Mr Brooke promises to do so. He writes to Ladislaw and invites him to stay at Tipton Grange, but he forgets to tell Dorothea what he has done. Mr Brooke has political ambitions and he thinks that Ladislaw could possibly edit the *Middlemarch Pioneer* which he has just bought.

COMMENTARY: We can see the careful planning that went into George Eliot's novels. No incident remains unexplained or without significance and no relationship is forced—each interrelationship is a logical consequence of incident and character; for example, a) through Mr Casaubon's heart attack, for which in many ways he had been prepared, George Eliot is able to link the two major plots, that of Dorothea and Lydgate; and b) Mr Brooke has already been presented as someone of a not particularly perceptive nature, and as a man with a particular view of the role of women in the society, and therefore it is quite logical that he should not tell Dorothea that he had invited Will 'for she was engaged with her husband, and [in his mind] these things were of no importance to her'.

NOTES AND GLOSSARY:

stethoscope: the reference to the stethoscope indicates how far ahead of his time Lydgate is. For further comment on this see the note on p. 904 of the Penguin edition of *Middlemarch*

Chapter 31

Fred goes to Stone Court to recuperate and Mrs Vincy goes with him as she wishes to keep him and Mary Garth apart. Mrs Bulstrode visits Mrs Plymdale and is surprised to hear that there is a great deal of gossip about her niece and Lydgate. She goes directly to Rosamond and asks her if she is engaged. Rosamond is embarrassed because she is not able to say that Lydgate has asked her to marry her though she believes he will. Mrs Bulstrode then asks her husband to find out if Lydgate intends to marry in the near future. When Lydgate says 'No' she goes to him and says he is being unfair to Rosamond because, as she tells him, 'Where you frequent a house it may militate very much against a girl's making a desirable settlement in life, and prevent her from accepting offers even if they are made'. Lydgate is angry at the gossip but decides not to see Rosamond. Ten days elapse during which time Rosamond is very unhappy. Then Mrs Vincy asks Lydgate to deliver a note to Mr Vincy. Lydgate goes to the house, finds Rosamond alone and when she weeps he is overcome and, believing himself to be in love with her, proposes marriage. That evening he asks for Mr Vincy's consent. Mr Vincy, who is in a good humour because he thinks Mr Featherstone is about to die and leave Fred Stone Court, agrees readily.

COMMENTARY: Lydgate proposes to Rosamond more out of pity than love. He tends to regard women as helpless creatures and it is not until he is married and it is too late that he realises that they can be otherwise.

NOTES AND GLOSSARY:

Orlandos: refers to the hero of Shakespeare's play *As You Like It*

lashed to the mast . . . . the sirens: in classical mythology the sirens were supposed to lure sailors to their death on the rocks. Ulysses lashed himself to the mast and was thus able to sail past them

stage Ariadne: in the Greek legend Ariadne helped Theseus kill the Minotaur (see note, Chapter 22). He swore eternal devotion but later left her. Rosamond sees herself as such a woman

---

Chapter 32

Peter Featherstone's health deteriorates and it becomes apparent that he will die soon. All his blood relations come to visit him. Their concern is not for Peter but for his money. They are particuarly anxious that he leaves it to them and not to the Vincys or Mary Garth. The Vincys and Mary Garth are admitted to the sick-room but Peter refuses to see his relatives, indeed, as he grows weaker, his dislike of them grows stronger.

COMMENTARY:The blood relatives are presented as human predators whose only concern is with money. Their attitude is just another instance of the greed and selfishness to be found in so many of the other characters.

NOTES AND GLOSSARY:

Brobdingnag specimens: gigantic examples of the type. Brobdingnag was the land of giants in Jonathan Swift's (1667-1745) *Gulliver's Travels* (1726)

Borrow: George Borrow (1803-81), author of *The Bible in Spain* (1841), an account of his adventures as travelling agent for the Bible Society

Three Crofts and the Manganese: firms in which Featherstone held shares

Blue-coat land: land on which a charitable institution will be built. In Blue Coat schools the pupils wore the almoner's blue coat; the most notable of these charitable schools is Christ's Hospital, now at Horsham, Sussex, founded in London by Edward VI, King of England (1547-53)

Peel, now Sir Robert: Sir Robert Peel (1788-1850) inherited the baronetcy on his father's death, 3 May 1830. He was Prime Minister from 1841 to 1847

Chapter 33

Mary is keeping watch over Mr Featherstone. At 3 a.m. he wakes up very clear-headed, and demands that Mary takes for herself the money from a tin box by his bedside and that she burns one of the two wills he has made. She refuses to do either and insists that he wait until daylight when there are other witnesses. When she wakes in the morning he is dead.

BOOK FOUR: THREE LOVE PROBLEMS

Chapter 34

Peter Featherstone had planned an elaborate funeral for himself and as a last act of spite against his relatives has invited them to attend it so as to make them think that they will be beneficiaries in his will.

Celia, Sir James, Mr Brooke and Dorothea observe the funeral from a window at Lowick Manor. Just as Mrs Cadwallader notices an ugly frog-faced stranger in the crowd Celia sees Will Ladislaw. This comes as a complete surprise to Dorothea and Mr Brooke hastily explains that he has invited Will as he hopes he will help him with his work. Casaubon has now joined the group and he immediately concludes that Mr Brooke had invited Will at Dorothea's request. As there are others present she is unable to explain to Casaubon that this is not so. Brooke tells Casaubon that Will has brought the Aquinas painting and he goes out to fetch Will and the painting.

COMMENTARY: This chapter indicates again the gap between the world of Tipton and Freshitt and the world outside. Appropriately enough, according to the social hierarchy of the time, the Chettams, the Brookes and Mrs Cadwallader look down from a height on the funeral procession and the people who attend it. Reference is made to the new manufacturing class, the Vincys, and the effect the new industry is having on the handloom weavers in Tipton and Freshitt. Mrs Cadwallader also has problems placing the rich Lowick farmers within the social hierarchy. As 'farmers without landlords' she can only describe them as 'monsters'. The Dorothea-Casaubon-Will plot is further strengthened.

NOTES AND GLOSSARY:

Harpagon: the miser in Molière's (name assumed by the French comic dramatist Jean Baptiste Poquelin, 1622-73) play *L'Avare* (1668) (*The Miser*)

A coursing fellow: that is, someone who hunts game, especially hares

Chapter 35

The Vincys, the Garths and Peter Featherstone's relatives, whom George Eliot describes as vultures, are gathered together to hear the reading of the will. All are surprised at the arrival of a stranger, Joshua Rigg. This is the man Mrs Cadwallader described as having a 'frog-face'. Mr Standish, the lawyer, reads the first will which leaves several hundred pounds to each of Peter's blood relations. The bulk of the money, ten thousand pounds, is left to Fred Vincy and the residue of personal property and land to Joshua Rigg. However, there is a second will and this revokes almost all the legacies. The property and land still go to Rigg but the money is to be used for the erection and endowment of almshouses for old men on a piece of land near Middlemarch. With the exception of Joshua Rigg all the expectant beneficiaries are bitter about this new will, none more so than Fred Vincy who tells Mary Garth he must now become a clergyman.

COMMENTARY: Once again George Eliot expresses her dislike of greed and selfishness and points out that people who possess these vices are likely to be disappointed.

NOTES AND GLOSSARY:
batrachian: frog-like
last bulletins . . . Duke of Clarence: the Duke became King William IV
                         on the death of George IV in 1830
loobies: country bumpkins

Chapter 36

Mr Vincy's disappointment that Fred has not inherited anything from Mr Featherstone turns into irritation with his children. He insists that Fred should give up his idle ways and he tells Rosamond that she should break the engagement with Lydgate, as the latter has no money. Rosamond is determined to marry Lydgate and finally gets her father's consent though he warns her that business is bad and he cannot provide money for the wedding. Both Lydgate and Rosamond spend more than they can afford. Lydgate has extravagant tastes and expects that Mr Vincy will provide a handsome dowry and Rosamond relies on Lydgate's wealthy and aristocratic relatives. She looks forward to the time when they are married and she can persuade Lydgate to move from the vulgar environment of Middlemarch. Lydgate looks forward to the marriage which he believes will bring peace, calm and order into his life and enable him to spent more time on his scientific experiments.

COMMENTARY: George Eliot introduces a theme in this chapter which was a major one in another of her novels, *Silas Marner*. This is the theme of the futility of an undue reliance on Providence or Chance. Fred, expecting to inherit Peter Featherstone's property, had not prepared himself for any occupation. Instead he hoped to lead a life of idle pleasure living off the profits of his inheritance. But, George Eliot points out, life is not like that. To a certain degree the same unthinking attitude is to be found in Rosamond and Lydgate. Both spend beyond their means without first ascertaining the true facts of their financial situation. Lydgate's naivety about such matters is paralleled by his naivety with regard to the female sex, a point already touched upon, and further emphasised by George Eliot in the last sentence of this chapter.

NOTES AND GLOSSARY:

Valenciennes: a very fine lace from the French town of that name

---

Chapter 37

Mr Brooke has bought a newspaper, the *Pioneer*, and hopes to use it to further his political career. Most people disapprove of this move and suggest that he apply his liberal ideas to his own tenants. Mr Brooke hopes that Will Ladislaw will edit the paper.

Will goes to see Dorothea and tells her about the project. She thinks it an excellent idea but has a feeling that Mr Casaubon might not agree. Will discusses his family with her and Dorothea reaches the conclusion that they have been badly treated by the Casaubons. When Mr Casaubon comes home she tells him of Will's plans. Mr Casaubon is extremely angry and writes to Will telling him not to accept the position and stating that if he does so he will no longer be welcome at Lowick Manor.

Dorothea continues to think of Will's family and decides that because they have been wronged by the Casaubon family Mr Casaubon should change his will and give to Will a portion of what he intends to bequeath to her. On hearing her proposal Mr Casaubon is very angry and tells Dorothea that he will not discuss the matter with her. He acknowledges that Dorothea has no ulterior motive for her suggestion but fears that his own position is being undermined by Will. Will replies to Casaubon, rejecting his demand that he refuse the job.

COMMENTARY: Dorothea's innocence (or naivety?) leads her to worsen the relationship between Mr Casaubon and Will Ladislaw. Mr Casaubon is further conscious of his failures and sees Will Ladislaw as a threat, though he refuses to acknowledge this. 'All through his life Mr Casaubon had been trying not to admit even to himself the inward sores of self-doubt and jealousy'.

NOTES AND GLOSSARY:

dark-blue freemen: dark blue was the colour used to signify one of the political parties. According to John Prest, Coventry was 'the only town where, before the Great Reform Bill, the election was fought between light and dark blue factions, and the results determined by the freemen'

Huskisson: William Huskisson (1770-1830), a Whig politician and a representative of the mercantile interests in Parliament

Delectus: an anthology of Greek or Latin passages used for translation purposes in the schools

Lowth: there are several theories about which Lowth is referred to here. Most critics conclude that the passage refers to Robert Lowth (1710-87), Bishop of London, Hebrew scholar and a man who engaged in controversy with Bishop Warburton (see note, Chapter 29)

Chapter 38

Tipton society is upset about Mr Brooke's political ambitions (he aims to be a Whig member of Parliament). They quite rightly point out to him that whilst he espouses the Liberal course his treatment of his tenants leaves much to be desired. Mr Brooke endeavours to defend himself but it is obvious that with regard to his tenants he is at fault.

COMMENTARY: George Eliot points out the hypocrisy of so-called reformers like Mr Brooke. She also shows us how narrow the Tipton society is by revealing its suspicion of Ladislaw because he has some foreign blood. This recalls the suspicion of the village community towards Silas Marner in the novel of the same name.

NOTES AND GLOSSARY:

Brougham and Useful Knowledge: Henry Brougham (1778-1868), radical politician and reformer. Partly responsible for founding the Society for the Diffusion of Useful Knowledge in 1825

modus: the money paid in lieu of a tithe

Lafitte: Jacques Lafitte (1767-1844), one of the leaders of the 1830 Revolution in France

The Edinburgh: *The Edinburgh Review*, founded in 1802, expressed Whig opinions

fiat justitia, ruat . . .: (*Latin*) let justice be done even if the heavens fall

Chapter 39

Sir James Chettam decides to enlist Dorothea's aid to persuade her uncle to improve the lot of his tenants. Dorothea goes to visit his uncle, and tells him that he cannot possibly enter Parliament as a reform candidate unless he makes reforms on his own estate. Mr Brooke will make no promises but says he will think about it. When he leaves the room to speak to the son of one of his tenants who has been caught poaching, Will and Dorothea are left alone and Will has the opportunity to tell Dorothea that Mr Casaubon has forbidden him to visit Lowick Manor.

Mr Brooke goes to visit Dagley, the father of the boy who has been caught poaching. Dagley, who is drunk, insults Mr Brooke and tells him that, when the Parliamentary reforms are made, landlords such as he will be punished. Mr Brooke is a little surprised as he thought the tenants liked him.

COMMENTARY: George Eliot was well aware of the deplorable living conditions of many of the tenant farmers. Her criticism of Mr Brooke could be extended to social criticism of all those landlords who lived in luxury and ignored the poverty of the people around them. Dorothea's genuine concern and awareness are in marked contrast to the hypocrisy and ignorance of Mr Brooke. ·

NOTES AND GLOSSARY:

Young: Edward Young (1683-1765), author of *The Complaint, or Night Thoughts*

Chapter 40

The scene shifts to the Garth household. Caleb receives a letter from Sir James Chettam offering him the management of Freshitt Hall and saying that Mr Brooke would also like him to take over Tipton Manor. The whole family is delighted, particularly Mary, as it means she can stay at home instead of taking up a teaching position at a school in York.

That evening Mr Farebrother visits them and tells them that Fred has decided to go back to university. Fred has not come himself as he is ashamed because he still owes Mr Garth money.

Later on Caleb thinks that Fred might like to become his assistant. Mrs Garth says that the Vincys will object because they will consider the job beneath Fred, and they will think that the Garths want Fred to marry Mary.

Mr Garth mentions that both Joshua Rigg and Mr Bulstrode have asked him for a valuation of Stone Court.

COMMENTARY: The happiness, honesty and simplicity of the Garth family are stressed and set in sharp contrast with the other households in the novel.

More links are made between the various characters, which in turn bring about the natural interaction of the various plots.

NOTES AND GLOSSARY:

Cincinnatus: a Roman hero and statesman (*c*.519BC-438BC). He was recalled from disgrace because he was the only man who could save the city

Chapter 41

Joshua Rigg is visited at Stone Court by John Raffles, his stepfather who wants some money. Rigg, remembering how cruelly Raffles had treated him as a child, reluctantly gives him a sovereign.

Raffles's brandy flask is loose in its covering and he picks up a piece of paper to wedge it tight. This is a letter from Nicholas Bulstrode.

COMMENTARY: The letter is mentioned twice and we can be certain that it will play a role in future events. The use of such a device is typical of nineteenth-century melodrama. Its purpose is to create suspense and to account for certain events which will follow.

NOTES AND GLOSSARY:

father-in-law: stepfather
Huskisson: William Huskisson (see note, Chapter 37) was killed at the opening of the Manchester and Liverpool railway on 15 September 1830

Chapter 42

Mr Casaubon is bitter about Will Ladislaw because he believes that Will ridicules his scholarly efforts in front of Dorothea, thus making Dorothea despise him. He decides that Will would be an unsuitable husband for Dorothea and determines to take steps to prevent such a thing happening should he die—and he is aware of the fact that this could happen.

In spite of the fact that Mr Casaubon never wants to hear the truth if it is unpalatable he decides to ask Lydgate how ill he is. He does this because he fears that he might die suddenly and he wants to ensure that his great work will be completed and published by someone else. And this of course must be prepared for. Lydgate tells him that he has a heart complaint, that he might live for another fifteen years but that he could die at any time.

After Lydgate leaves, Dorothea, conscious of the fact that Lydgate has probably told Mr Casaubon just how serious his illness is, joins him in the garden in order to comfort him. Casaubon rejects her and Dorothea retreats in anger. Later in the evening her anger subsides, and she goes once more to Casaubon and they retire in peace together.

COMMENTARY: Once again George Eliot emphasises the increasing disenchantment of Casaubon and Dorothea with one another and with their marriage. For Mr Casaubon 'the young creature who had worshipped him with perfect trust had quickly turned into the critical wife'. For Dorothea the man whom she believed to possess great intellect, who, she hoped, would help her to enlarge her own, had turned into a petty failure incapable of admitting his own mediocrity. It is a tribute to George Eliot's insight into character that she provides perfect psychological reasons for the mutual misunderstanding. Whilst showing a degree of sympathy based on understanding for Casaubon, she makes it quite clear that Dorothea's honesty and generosity are to be preferred.

NOTES AND GLOSSARY:

sciolism: a pretentious smattering of knowledge
Laennec: René Théophile Laennec (1781-1826), French physician

BOOK FIVE: THE DEAD HAND

Chapter 43

Dorothea wonders about Mr Casaubon's changed attitude. He now discusses his work with her and has strange moods. She decides to ask Dr Lydgate what passed between him and her husband and she drives to his house to see him. Lydgate is not in, but his wife, Rosamond, is there and so too is Will Ladislaw. Dorothea leaves almost immediately to seek Lydgate out at the hospital. On her way there she realises that she left abruptly not only because she felt guilty about seeing Will when she knows her husband disapproves, but also because she felt a pang of jealousy when she saw Rosamond and Ladislaw together.

Will is angry that he has been caught in what may be looked upon as compromising circumstances.

When Lydgate returns home he tells Rosamond that Dorothea will make a bequest to the hospital and she tells him that Will adores Dorothea.

NOTES AND GLOSSARY:

Imogene: the heroine of Shakespeare's *Cymbeline*
Cato's daughter: Portia in Shakespeare's *Julius Caesar*

leather and prunella: the cobbler's apron was made of leather, the clergyman's gown of prunella. The phrase is an expression for something to which one is entirely indifferent and indicates that Ladislaw cares nothing for social distinction

Chapter 44

Dorothea goes to see Lydgate at the hospital, and, after telling her of his conversation with Mr Casaubon, Lydgate goes on to discuss the New Hospital. He tells her that the other doctors in Middlemarch are opposed to it because of their dislike of Bulstrode, whose idea it is, and also of Lydgate himself because he is a stranger and because he is trying to introduce new medical methods. 'There is no stifling the offence of being young, and a new-comer, and happening to know something more than the old inhabitants.' Dorothea is indignant that the doctors should take this attitude and tells Lydgate that she can probably spare two hundred pounds a year for the hospital.

COMMENTARY (Chapters 43-4): In these two chapters George Eliot contrasts both the looks and attitudes of Rosamond and Dorothea. Rosamond's main interests are clothes and social position whilst Dorothea continues to show a genuine concern for mankind. It is this concern that creates her association with Lydgate and at the same time links the two major plots in the novel.

Chapter 45

Lydgate makes many enemies in Middlemarch. There are various reasons for this: first, the medical practitioners, as well as the lay people, regard his new methods with suspicion; second, the other doctors envy him his successes and feel he is trying to make fools of them. They also feel he is arrogant and lacks due respect for his elders and betters. Third, his association with Bulstrode, whom they regard as a religious hypocrite, makes them regard him as a medical charlatan.

Lydgate discusses the antagonism of the others with Farebrother and the latter tells him that he will weather the storm if he is prudent. Farebrother also advises Lydgate that he should have as little to do with Bulstrode as possible and that he should avoid getting into debt. Rosamond regrets the fact that Lydgate is a doctor.

COMMENTARY: 'You'll weather it if you are prudent'. This is Farebrother's advice to Lydgate but unfortunately for Lydgate prudence is a virtue he lacks, and this lack could perhaps be called his 'fatal flaw'. When the others accuse him of arrogance they are in some ways correct (see Ch. 17). He has a firm belief in his own methods and does not easily tolerate fools. His naivité with regard to women also extends to the rest of mankind. If the cause is just and right then he believes that all must be well.

NOTES AND GLOSSARY:

Burke and Hare: a notorious pair of Edinburgh criminals who murdered people to obtain corpses for dissection by doctors. Hare turned Crown witness and Burke was hanged in January 1829

St John Long: a notorious quack doctor who was tried for manslaughter in 1830

Raspail: François Raspail (1794-1878), French naturalist and political reformer

Vesalius: Andrea Vesalius (1514-64), a pioneer in anatomy

Galen: a celebrated Greek physician of the second century

Chapter 46

The talk in Middlemarch is very much about the Reform Bill. Mr Brooke still pursues his political ambitions and supports the reform side though with some reservations. Will is enjoying his job as editor of the *Pioneer* and has become genuinely interested in the political situation. He is regarded with suspicion by most of the people of Middlemarch essentially because they think of him as a 'foreigner'. The Lydgates remain his best friends. One evening he and Lydgate almost quarrel over the question of the ethics of supporting a cause when aid for this cause is given by undesirable people. Lydgate thinks of Brooke in connection with Will and Will thinks of Bulstrode in connection with Lydgate. When Will leaves it is revealed that the real reason for Lydgate's irritation is that he has had a letter demanding payment for the furniture that he bought. Rosamond is pregnant.

COMMENTARY: George Eliot is sharply critical of Mr Brooke, who is interested 'not [in] ideas . . . but a way of putting them'. He supports the reform side not out of a genuine concern for reform but out of self-interest and personal ambition.

In this chapter she also raises the question of whether the ends justify the means. Lydgate believes 'that a man may work for a special end with others whose motives and general course are equivocal, if he is quite sure of his personal independence'. But as was pointed out earlier (see commentary on chapters 25-6), 'No man is an island'. Society and other men will impose restrictions, no matter how we strain for the opposite, our human lots are 'woven and interwoven' (Chapter 15).

NOTES AND GLOSSARY:

Lord John Russell: his bill for electoral reform was introduced in March 1831. Parliament was dissolved in April 1831. See note on 'Politics and the political system' in Part 3

political unions: several associations were set up in the early 1830s with the aim of bringing about electoral reform. See note on 'Politics and the political system' in Part 3

Burke: Edmund Burke (1729-97), a famous Whig politician

energumen: a fanatical devotee

galligaskins: breeches or gaiters

Stanley: Lord Stanley (1799-1869), 14th Earl of Derby, Chief Secretary for Ireland and later Prime Minister

Chapter 47

That evening Will reflects on his motives for staying on in Middlemarch and admits to himself that he remains there because of Dorothea. However, Mr Casaubon is wrong in thinking that Will plans to marry Dorothea when Mr Casaubon dies. He prefers her to remain as she is and takes a certain delight in the special feelings and devotion he has for her, which he regards as being of the same order as the love Dante had for Beatrice and Petrarch for Laura. However, he is irritated at not being able to see her and decides to go to church at Lowich the next day. He goes in good spirits but when he gets there he realises he has made a mistake. He is embarrassed throughout the service and leaves without speaking to Dorothea.

COMMENTARY: Will is described as good-natured but a little juvenile. He goes to the church service partly to see Dorothea and partly because he thinks it might be fun to irritate Mr Casaubon. Only too late does he realise his mistake. It is incidents like this one that help him to mature.

There is also an indication in this chapter that the social changes which were affecting the towns had yet to be felt in the villages. Even in 1831 Lowick was at peace, 'not more agitated by Reform than by the solemn tenor of the Sunday sermon'.

NOTES AND GLOSSARY:

old Drayton: Michael Drayton (1563-1631), the poet

Chapter 48

Dorothea had hoped that Mr Casaubon would speak to Will and that friendly relations would be resumed between the two men. She realises now that this will not happen and is extremely depressed. She had hoped for a richer, fuller life and companionship and now she feels that she will continue to live more and more in a virtual 'tomb'.

That evening Mr Casaubon asks her to help with the organisation of his notes. During the night she wakes and finds him sitting by the fire. He asks her to continue working for an hour. He then asks her if she will promise in the event of his death to 'avoid doing what I should deprecate, and apply [herself] to do what I should desire'. Dorothea is reluctant to promise for she feels that what he asks of her is that she should continue his work and she feels unwilling to condemn herself for the rest of her life to sorting out 'shattered mummies . . . crushed ruins'.

When she wakes the next morning, she decides that in spite of her feelings she must fulfil her wifely duties and goes to tell Casaubon so. However, when she finds him, he is dead.

COMMENTARY: Dorothea's decision to obey Casaubon emphasises her strong sense of duty. Her action stands out in marked contrast to Rosamond's.

NOTES AND GLOSSARY:

Lavoisier: Antoine Lavoisier (1743-94), the famous French chemist

Gog and Magog: mythical beings mentioned in the Bible (Revelation 20:8) who found their way into medieval legends

Chapter 49

The day after Casaubon's funeral Sir James Chettam and Mr Brooke are discussing Will Ladislaw. We know it has something to do with Casaubon's will, but we are not told what. Sir James believes that Will's presence in Middlemarch compromises Dorothea and demands that Mr Brooke dismiss Ladislaw and send him away. Mr Brooke refuses to do this on two grounds. First because he needs Will's help and second because he says that if he were to send Will away (and this is not possible because Will is a free man) it would look as if Casaubon had reasons for his suspicions.

COMMENTARY:The quarrel between Sir James and Mr Brooke about whether Ladislaw should be sent away or remain in Middlemarch reveals how both are motivated by self-interest and, coming directly after the previous chapter, serves to highlight Dorothea's unselfishness. George Eliot creates dramatic suspense by hinting at the fact that the reason for the argument has something to do with Casaubon's will without telling the readers just what it is.

NOTES AND GLOSSARY:
Thoth and Dagon: Thoth is an Egyptian god, Dagon a Philistine one
Norfolk Island: a British penal settlement off the coast of Australia

---

Chapter 50

Dorothea goes to stay with Celia at Freshitt Hall. When she recovers Dorothea is anxious to return to Lowick Manor and look into Mr Casaubon's affairs; 'he has perhaps made some addition to his will'. The reason why everyone tries to prevent her from returning is that Mr Casaubon has indeed made an addition to his will but not what Dorothea expects. Celia tells her what it is. Mr Casaubon has left all his property to her but has added a codicil saying she loses everything if she marries Will. Celia assures her that no one would suspect her of wanting to marry Ladislaw for as 'Mrs Cadwallader said you might as well marry an Italian with white mice'.

This codicil makes Dorothea lose all respect for Mr Casaubon and turns her thoughts in the direction of Will Ladislaw. She seeks advice about who should have the living at Lowick parish. Lydgate suggests that she consider the Rev. Farebrother. This is partly to make amends for his previous treatment of Farebrother.

COMMENTARY: Dorothea's genuine concern and consideration are again contrasted with the self-interest and egoism not only of Casaubon but also of her relatives. The real reason why Mr Brooke refuses to dismiss Ladislaw is because he needs him. The others want him to leave, partly because his presence might damage the family name, partly because of his politics, and partly because they are afraid he might marry Dorothea and then the money would be lost to the family.

There is an indication of Lydgate's growing awareness when he says to Dorothea 'I find myself that it's uncommonly difficult to make the right thing work; there are so many strings pulling at once'. There is also a note of dramatic irony when he describes Farebrother. 'He has neither venom nor doubleness in him, and those often go with a more correct outside' (compare him with Bulstrode).

NOTES AND GLOSSARY:
Latimer: Archbishop Latimer (1485-1555), famous for the simple, homely style of his sermons

Chapter 51

Ladislaw is unaware of the codicil in Casaubon's will. However he can see that many, including Dorothea's family, would look upon any overture he might make to Dorothea as the advances of a poor man trying to gain the favour and fortune of a rich woman.

Mr Brooke makes a disastrous election speech and ruins any hopes of his entering Parliament. He withdraws his candidature, sells the *Pioneer* and dismisses Will, now that he no longer has any need of him. Will sees this as a move to force him to leave Middlemarch but he determines to remain there until he chooses to leave. Before he leaves he hopes for a sign from Dorothea that she might accept a proposal from him should he be able to make a success of his life in the next few years. He plans a political career.

COMMENTARY: 'When I give a vote I must know what I'm doing; I must look to what will be the effects on my till and ledger'. Mawnsey represents the small traders and retailers of the time whose interests were in profits, not reform. Then, as now, the small businessman was likely to be conservative.

NOTES AND GLOSSARY:

Parliamentary Candidate Society: presumably an association similar to the political unions

plumpers: people who voted twice for one candidate

ten-pound householders: one of the points in the Reform Act was that people who occupied property valued at ten pounds or more were entitled to vote in the borough elections

the new police: Sir Robert Peel founded the first police force in 1829. Hence the nickname of 'Bobbies' for English policemen; they were also called 'peelers'

eating his dinners: studying law. A student's attendance at the Inns of Court and at some colleges was counted by the number of occasions he dined in hall

Althorpe: Viscount Althorpe (1782-1845), the man largely responsible for procuring the passage of the Reform Bill through Parliament

Chapter 52

The Farebrother family are overjoyed that Mr Farebrother is to be the new Rector at Lowick. His sister says he must marry now and suggests he think of Mary Garth. Mr Farebrother is not averse to that idea.

The next week, however, Fred Vincy comes to see him. Fred has passed his university examinations and has even resigned himself to becoming a clergyman. But Mary Garth once told him that she would never marry him if he did. He asks Mr Farebrother to approach Mary on his behalf to see if she still feels the same way and if there is any chance for him. With mixed feelings Mr Farebrother tells Mary all of this. Mary reiterates what she said before. She will never marry Fred if he enters the Church. She is willing to marry him, indeed she will never marry anyone else, but not until he has proved himself. Mr Farebrother realises there is no hope for himself.

Chapter 53

Joshua Rigg had always wanted to be a money-changer. Therefore fifteen months after he inherited Stone Court from his father he sold it to Mr Bulstrode, who intended to live there when he retired. One evening when Bulstrode is discussing his property with Caleb Garth, Raffles appears once more. It is evident to Caleb that, even if they are very different, Raffles and Bulstrode know one another. Raffles and Bulstrode go back to Stone Court and it becomes obvious that Raffles knows something about Bulstrode that enables him to blackmail him. Raffles agrees to leave if Bulstrode gives him two hundred pounds but he refuses to promise that he will never return. Before he leaves he mentions the daughter and child of 'the old widow' Bulstrode married. What he does not tell Bulstrode is that the name of the man the daughter married was Ladislaw.

COMMENTARY: We now see the significance of the scrap of paper that Raffles unwittingly picked up last time he was at Stone Court. It has led him to Bulstrode, a man over whom he has a hold, though at this stage we are not told what this hold is. This is George Eliot's method of creating suspense and retaining our interest in the events to come. There is a hint that when all is revealed Ladislaw will be involved in some way but it is nothing more than a hint. What she has done is create a further interweaving of plots and interdependence of characters.

NOTES AND GLOSSARY:
'read himself': read and assented to the Thirty-nine Articles
Warren Hastings: (1732-1818), first Governor-General of India. He was tried for corruption but acquitted in 1795 after a trial lasting seven years
in the Dissenting line: belonging to the non-conformist church which was considered socially inferior to the Church of England

BOOK SIX: THE WIDOW AND THE WIFE

Chapter 54

Against the advice and wishes of her relatives and friends Dorothea returns to Lowick Manor. She is anxious to see Will but believes he is avoiding her because he knows of the codicil.

One morning Tantripp announces that Will has come to see her. Will, who does not know about the codicil, has come to say goodbye. Both sense an emotional attachment to each other but because of a series of misundertandings they do not say what they want to say. Sir James Chettam arrives. His obvious dislike of Will wounds the latter's pride and makes him determined to leave Dorothea in peace.

COMMENTARY: Through her psychological insight into character, as well as by withholding complete knowledge of the situation from the characters involved, George Eliot accounts perfectly well for the actions and misunderstandings of Dorothea and Will. Will's departure is explained, we are left wondering about the outcome, and the stage is cleared for a return to other characters and plots in the novel.

Compare also Dorothea's growing awareness that the shaping of one's life is not just the matter of will she thought it was: 'I used to despise women a little for not shaping their lives more', with the like awareness that Lydgate expressed in Chapter 50 (see commentary).

Chapter 55

Dorothea is sad when Will leaves but she does not recognise that her sadness stems from the fact that she loves him. This realisation is still to come.

One evening she goes to Freshitt Hall. Mrs Cadwallader is there and the conversation turns to second marriages. Later that evening Dorothea informs Celia that she has no intention of marrying again. Instead she intends to continue with her earlier plan for the cottages and she is going to ask Caleb Garth to advise her.

NOTES AND GLOSSARY:

Dido or Zenobia: in classical mythology Dido was queen of Carthage and Zenobia queen of Palmyra. Both women wielded political power and resisted the attempt of men to take it from them

Chapter 56

Dorothea employs Caleb and they are both impressed by one another. The railway is coming to Middlemarch and there is much superstitious opposition to it, particularly on the part of the cottagers, women, and some landholders. One morning Caleb Garth comes across a group of farmers attacking some railway surveyors. He goes to the aid of the railway employees and the farmers knock down and injure his assistant. At that moment Fred Vincy is riding by wondering what he is to do with his life. He comes to Caleb's rescue. When the farmers have been pacified Fred offers to help Caleb in place of his injured assistant. When they finish work Fred asks Caleb if he will take him on as an assistant. He also tells Caleb that he loves Mary and feels that she might marry him if he can make a success of his life. Caleb tells Fred to see him next morning in his office. He has, however, already decided to employ Fred. Mrs Garth is disappointed as she hoped Mary would marry Mr Farebrother.

The next morning Caleb tells Fred he will employ him. Fred goes to break the news to his father. Mr Vincy is disappointed as he feels he has wasted money on Fred's education; he had hoped for a higher social position for him. However, he accepts Fred's decision. Mrs Vincy is very upset as she too had hoped for a much higher social position for Fred; she is convinced now that Fred will marry Mary Garth and she is very opposed to this. Mr Vincy tells her she must make the most of the situation. He also hints that Lydgate's practice is going badly and that Lydgate is in debt.

COMMENTARY: The railway incident once more places the novel within a social, historical period. It also provides another instance of how George Eliot uses each incident to create a logical development in the plot—in this case Fred's meeting with Mr Garth and the injury of the latter's assistant which means he needs Fred's help.

NOTES AND GLOSSARY:

hundred: sub-division of a county

clemmin':   (*dialect*) starving

Chapter 57

Fred Vincy is going to visit Mary Garth who is staying at Lowick Parsonage. On the way he calls in to see Mrs Garth. She is obviously not pleased that Fred wants to marry Mary, and lets him know that if he was not around Mary could have married Mr Farebrother, a marriage which she considers to be infinitely superior. Fred is astonished at this piece of news. He feels jealous and also certain that he will lose, because Mary must consider Mr Farebrother a much better match.

When he sees Mary at the parsonage it is obvious to her that there is something wrong. When he has a brief chance to be alone with her he tells her of his fears that she will marry Mr Farebrother because he is a much better man. Mary is astonished that Mr Farebrother is seriously interested in her and in a subtle way indicates that Fred is the man she loves.

NOTES AND GLOSSARY:

a regenerate Porson: Richard Porson (1759–1808), the Greek scholar who was overfond of drink

making a meal of a nightingale: having the best things in life

---

Chapter 58

Lydgate's cousin has come to stay with them. He is stupid and boring but because of her snobbery Rosamond is impressed by him. He invites her to go riding with him, and, despite the fact that Lydgate has forbidden her to ride because of her pregnancy, she disobeys him and goes. There is a minor accident which leads to Rosamond's losing her baby.

Lydgate has other problems. He has sunk more and more into debt and has realised that he must take severe measures both to try and pay his present debts, and not to incur any more. He will take a security on their furniture, return some of the plate and try to reduce their standard of living. Up until now he has not told Rosamond of their financial difficulties. When he does so she shows a complete lack of sympathy and no real comprehension of the situation.

COMMENTARY: Lydgate's disenchantment, and, along with it, an increasing awareness, are carried one step further in this chapter. He realises that Rosamond has no interest at all in his concerns, that in fact what attracted her to him was his connection to nobility. 'Between him and her . . . there was that total missing of each other's mental track'. Instead of a loving wife who will obey him and support him in times of trouble he finds that he has married a wilful, obstinate woman whose only interests are her own selfish ones. He cannot help comparing her attitude with that of Dorothea. The loving self-sacrifice and devotion of Dorothea stand out in strong contrast to Rosamond's selfish remark 'What can *I* do'. The sense of values of the two women are also sharply contrasted. Rosamond's sole purpose in life is to climb up the social scale and lead a life of pleasure and luxury; if she takes pains it is 'with her music and the careful selection of her lace'. Dorothea's concern on the other hand is with improving the lot of the cottagers (see her remark to Mr Garth in Chapter 56). Dorothea's and Lydgate's positions are similar in that they both discover that the ideal person each thought they were marrying falls far short of the mark. Lydgate's position, however, is more tragic.

NOTES AND GLOSSARY:

Mechanics' Institute: these Institutes, started in the 1820s, were places where the working men could receive an education after work

Chapter 59

Fred Vincy hears about the codicil to Casaubon's will. He happens to mention it to Rosamond who in turn tells Lydgate. The latter tells her not to tell Ladislaw of it but as usual she ignores him and tells Will. This shocks Will, who leaves in a daze declaring he will never marry. Rosamond is irritated, not only because of Will's reaction but also because, in spite of Lydgate's order not to do so, she has asked her father for money and he has refused, saying he is likely to need money himself.

COMMENTARY: The way Will eventually hears about the codicil shows how all the events and persons in the novel are linked in some way or other.

Chapter 60

Mr Borthrop Trumbull conducts a large auction in Middlemarch. Mr Bulstrode, who now owns the *Pioneer*, asks Will to go to the auction and bid for a painting that Mrs Bulstrode wants. Will is planning to leave Middlemarch but not before he has seen Dorothea once more. He goes to the auction and buys the painting. A stranger, who turns out to be John Raffles, approaches him and asks him if his mother's name was Sarah Dunkirk. Will says 'Yes'. Later that evening Raffles meets him once more and tells him that the reason why his mother ran away from home was because her parents were receivers of stolen goods. Ladislaw wonders what Sir James and the others would have to say if they knew about this.

NOTES AND GLOSSARY:

Guido: probably Guido Reni (1575–1642), sixteenth-century Italian religious painter. The low price offered indicates that is was probably not an authentic Guido

'Berghems': Nicholas Berghem (1620–83), Dutch painter

rebus: a puzzle in which a word or phrase has to be guessed from pictures or diagrams that suggest the syllables that make up the word

a young Slender: a foolish young man. The name of a character in Shakespeare's *The Merry Wives of Windsor*

Chapter 61

This chapter takes up the events discussed in Chapter 53. Raffles has come once more to torment Mr Bulstrode and obtain more money from him. Mr Bulstrode is greatly disturbed, and his thoughts turn to his past. We learn that he was an orphan, educated at a charity school, that he became a clever but poor clerk, and that he was a member of the Dissenting church and was renowned for his religious zeal. The richest member of the congregation was Mr Dunkirk and when a vacancy occurred he offered Bulstrode a position with the firm. Bulstrode soon realised that Mr Dunkirk's business was an illegal one even though on the surface it appeared very respectable. He was a pawnbroker and his money was made through receiving stolen goods. This knowledge gave Bulstrode religious scruples, but his desire for wealth triumphed and he continued working for Mr Dunkirk. Mr Dunkirk's son died and then Mr Dunkirk died also. Mrs Dunkirk, who was a simple, honest woman without knowledge of the true source of her wealth, agreed to marry Bulstrode but not before an attempt had been made to find her daughter who had run away from home when she learnt about her father's criminal activities. She went on the stage and later married a Polish emigré, Will's father. Bulstrode actually finds out her whereabouts but withholds the knowledge from Mrs Dunkirk as he fears she will give part of the family wealth to her daughter and he wishes to retain it all for himself. The only other person who knows these facts is Raffles. This explains his hold over Bulstrode. Bulstrode married Mrs Dunkirk, justifying his actions by arguing that he would use the money to promote Christian actions and glorify God whereas others might waste it. 'Who would use money and position better than he meant to use them?' Some years later Mrs Dunkirk died and left him a hundred thousand pounds. It was with this money that he moved to Middlemarch and established himself as a banker and a promoter of good works. That was over thirty years ago.

Now his past, in the form of Raffles, has come back to torment him. Whilst he cannot be prosecuted legally he feels that his past will be disclosed and he will be disgraced in the presence of his neighbours and his own wife. Apart from anything else he has a genuine spiritual need to make amends (he fears God's revenge) and so he decides to offer Ladislaw five hundred pounds a year and a proportion of his money when he dies. He asks Ladislaw to come and see him, tells him of the past and his present decision. Ladislaw refuses the money as he will have nothing to do with anything that might stain his honour. Bulstrode is both relieved (for he knows Will will not reveal what he has been told) and humiliated by Will's scornful refusal.

COMMENTARY: This chapter is essentially concerned with the character of Bulstrode and with George Eliot's interest in the motives of human actions.

Chapter 62

Will plans to leave Middlemarch immediately but wishes to see Dorothea before he leaves. He writes her a letter but on that particular day she has gone to Tipton Grange to prepare the house for her uncle's return. She calls at Freshitt Hall on the way. There Sir James, in the hope of discouraging her relationship with Will, persuades Mrs Cadwallader to suggest that Will is interested in Rosamond. Dorothea defends Will and declares this to be false gossip. When she arrives at Tipton she finds Will there. As on the previous occasion, they are involved in a series of misunderstandings and fail to understand one another's true feelings. After Will leaves, somewhat angry and convinced that Dorothea scorns him, Dorothea realises that Will was professing his love for her and not Rosamond. This makes her happy though she sees no chance of marriage between them.

COMMENTARY: Once again it is revealed how carefully George Eliot builds up her plots so that every incident and every attitude is accounted for. If Mrs Cadwallader had not repeated the gossip about Will and Rosamond Dorothea would have accepted at once that Will was talking about her. This would have created a different response in her and as a consequence in Will. Instead a series of misunderstandings is created, the relationship between Dorothea and Will is still not resolved and we, the readers, are kept in suspense.

It becomes perfectly reasonable for Will to disappear from the stage for the moment so that our attention can be turned once more to the other characters and plots within the novel.

NOTES AND GLOSSARY:
weepers: the black veil that widows wore in those days

BOOK SEVEN: TWO TEMPTATIONS

Chapter 63

Mr Farebrother has heard rumours that Lydgate is living beyond his means and that his practice is declining. He has also noted a change of attitude in Lydgate.

The Vincys hold a party on New Year's Day. Mr Farebrother notices that Rosamond's attitude towards her husband is correct but cool. Fred has insisted that his mother invite Mary Garth and when Mrs Vincy sees how fond her younger children are of Mary she says that she must come again. The three women of the Farebrother household still hope that their brother will marry Mary and Fred is still jealous of him. Farebrother decides to offer his help to Lydgate. He introduces the subject by thanking Lydgate for the favour he did him by pleading his cause with Dorothea. Lydgate realises that Farebrother is offering help and friendship but his pride is such that he refuses help and rebuffs Farebrother rather coldly.

COMMENTARY: George Eliot again shows the destructive role played by pride—in this case Lydgate's. She introduces another of her favourite topics, the question of Chance, and Mr Farebrother's remark, 'It's a rather strong check to one's self-complacency to find how much of one's right doing depends on not being in want of money' can be looked upon as a further plea on George Eliot's part to have some compassion for Bulstrode, particularly as it comes so soon after the chapter on the banker.

NOTES AND GLOSSARY:

tic-douloureux: a twitching caused by nervous tension
a Ken and a Tillotson: Bishop Ken (1637–1711) and Archbishop
              Tillotson (1630–94), eminent churchmen

Chapter 64

Lydgate now needs a hundred pounds to clear his debts. There are two other things that cause him distress apart from his debts. The first is the realisation that he is wasting the talent he has, the second is Rosamond's stubborn and selfish obstinacy and the fear that their love will be destroyed. He reflects bitterly on the fact that 'His marriage would be a mere piece of bitter irony if they could not go on loving each other'. Rosamond remains 'utterly aloof from him'. She refuses to help him or see how serious the situation is. Her only concern is with her own comfort and her determination to maintain her position in society and live in a grand manner. She places all the blame on Lydgate. He tells her that they must move to a cheaper house and that he has asked Trumbull to try to lease their house to Ned Plymdale, an old suitor of Rosamond's. Rosamond goes behind his back and tells Trumbull not to lease the house. When Lydgate finds out he is furious. He realises that he cannot make Rosamond see reason and he begins to dread her 'quiet elusive obstinacy'. In spite of his great reluctance to do so he feels that he must approach his uncle and ask if he can help him. Unknown to Lydgate Rosamond has already written to Sir Godwin asking for help.

COMMENTARY: George Eliot points to the destructive nature of money and what the need of it will lead men to. 'Doubtless [Lydgate's troubles] were sordid . . . there is no escape from the sordidness but by being free from money-craving'. Lydgate 'who had long ago determined to live aloof from such abject calculations' is now forced to realise that this is not possible. The man, whose 'conceit was of the arrogant sort' (Chapter 16) is being taught a lesson in humility.

There is bitter irony in Rosamond's statement 'appearances [have] very little to do with happiness'. The statement of course is true.

Chapter 65

Eventually a letter, addressed to Lydgate, arrives from his uncle, Sir Godwin Lydgate. Sir Godwin refuses to help and expresses contempt for Lydgate because he believes that Lydgate has been too cowardly to write himself. Lydgate is once more furious with Rosamond but realises that it seems impossible to change her or make her see reason.

COMMENTARY: Once more Rosamond reveals herself as totally selfish and insensitive. Lydgate is frustrated by his inability to make her understand or care. He can foresee the breakdown of their love and dreads a future in which he would 'sink into the hideous fettering of domestic hate'.

Chapter 66

Lydgate goes to the Green Dragon to see Bambridge about selling his horse. Desperate for money he begins to play billiards. Fred Vincy is surprised to see Lydgate gambling and tries to find an excuse to get him to leave. Such an excuse is provided when Mr Farebrother calls and asks to see Fred. Fred uses this opportunity to suggest to Lydgate that he too might like to see Mr Farebrother. Lydgate is happy to stop gambling and leaves after saying goodnight to Mr Farebrother. The Vicar warns Fred about taking up his old ways for he tells him that if he does so he may lose Mary Garth. Fred recognises the generosity behind the vicar's warning and resolves to mend his ways.

NOTES AND GLOSSARY:

twice-blessed mercy: refers to Shakespeare's *The Merchant of Venice*. Mercy is twice blessed because 'It blesseth him that gives and him that takes' (IV.1.185)

Chapter 67

Lydgate now sees that his only hope is to ask Bulstrode to lend him money. An opportunity comes when Bulstrode summons him. Bulstrode announces that he intends to leave Middlemarch and to withdraw his support from the hospital. There is a possibility that Mrs Casaubon might replace him but this is still not certain. Lydgate tells Bulstrode of his financial problems and asks for help. Bulstrode ignores Lydgate's appeal and advises him to declare himself bankrupt.

COMMENTARY: Once again Lydgate's illusion of independence is destroyed. The selfishness of his wife has led him to a state of bankruptcy and he is forced to seek aid from a man he despises. What makes it worse is that Lydgate has always prided himself on the fact that he was totally independent of Bulstrode. More and more he is coming to realise that acts which at one stage seemed 'impossible' become under different circumstances 'manifestly possible'.

NOTES AND GLOSSARY:
Philistine: an uncultured person

Chapter 68

This chapter moves back in time. Raffles returns to Middlemarch on Christmas Eve. Bulstrode looks after him for the evening and the next morning drives him to Ilsely. He gives Raffles money and tells him that he will supply him with more on condition that Raffles never returns to Middlemarch. However, he warns Raffles that if he returns he will get no more money.

Bulstrode fears exposure and makes plans to leave Middlemarch. These include asking Caleb Garth to manage his affairs including the running of Stone Court. Caleb suggests that Fred Vincy manage it and Bulstrode agrees.

COMMENTARY: This chapter explains Bulstrode's action in the previous chapter and shows what far-reaching effects a chain of events, once set in motion, can have on the lives of people who seemingly have no connection with one another—in this case Raffles and Lydgate.

Chapter 69

On the same day that Bulstrode has refused to help Lydgate Caleb Garth comes to see him. Garth informs Bulstrode that he found Raffles wandering ill by the wayside and that he has taken him to Stone Court. He also informs Bulstrode that he can no longer work for him. Bulstrode surmises correctly that Raffles has told Garth about Bulstrode's past and asks Garth to reconsider his decision. Garth refuses to do so but reassures Bulstrode that he will not repeat what Raffles has told him. Bulstrode sends for Lydgate to attend Raffles and sets out for Stone Court. Lydgate arrives eventually and after examining Raffles tells Bulstrode that he thinks Raffles will recover.

Bulstrode says he will stay with Raffles and Lydgate leaves strict instructions about the medical treatment. When Lydgate returns home he finds the creditors occupying his house and Rosamond in tears. He breaks down and asks Rosamond to love him. As usual she ignores his pleas and is offended when he suggests ironically that if she waits a day or two before going to her parents he might break his neck and then she could claim insurance.

COMMENTARY: Raffles's illness strengthens the Bulstrode-Lydgate connection. The chapter also shows Lydgate's continuing awareness of how little he and Rosamond have in common. And he can see clearly the consequences of this. In Chapter 67 George Eliot has pointed out that, given certain circumstances, 'the act which they [men] had called impossible . . . is becoming manifestly possible'. We are reminded of this statement in Chapter 70 when Lydgate reflects on 'that contrast in himself which a few months had brought—that he should be overjoyed at being under a strong personal obligation—that he should be overjoyed at getting money for himself from Bulstrode'.

NOTES AND GLOSSARY:

such large blue-bottles: large flies that throng around dirt. Here they symbolise the people who gather round when there is a chance of receiving a legacy

Dr Ware: author of *History and Treatment of Delirium Tremens* (1831). As it was first published in the USA it is unlikely that Lydgate would have heard of it at this time

Chapter 70

Lydgate has given Bulstrode instructions that Raffles must have no alcohol—the only thing he must be given is opium. Bulstrode obeys Lydgate's instructions although he wants Raffles to die. He fears what Raffles may say to Lydgate and regrets his refusal of Lydgate's request for a loan. The next day when Lydgate comes Bulstrode tells him that he has reconsidered his decision and will lend him a thousand pounds. Lydgate is overjoyed, and, though he is uneasy in his mind, he is too much relieved to think more about it.

The next evening Bulstrode asks Mrs Abel to watch over Raffles. When she comes to Bulstrode and suggests that she give Raffles a drink Bulstrode says nothing but gives her the key to the drink cabinet. When Lydgate comes the next day he is surprised to find Raffles on the point of death. He wonders if his instructions have been obeyed but decides he cannot question Bulstrode.

Mr Farebrother has heard about the creditors in Lydgate's house and once more comes to offer help. This time Lydgate is grateful but tells Farebrother his problems have been solved because of the loan from Bulstrode. Farebrother is worried, as he had warned Lydgate not to put himself in Bulstrode's debt.

Chapter 71

Mr Bambridge is lounging outside the Green Dragon. When Mr Bulstrode passes by he is reminded of a story Raffles told him at the horse fair at Bilkley. He repeats this story to the group who are with him and soon the whole town is gossiping about Bulstrode, and Lydgate's connection with him. Although they cannot prove anything against Lydgate they are sure Bulstrode gave him the thousand pounds as a bribe. There is a meeting of the Town Council at which Bulstrode's resignation from all public positions is called for. Bulstrode is on the point of collapse and Lydgate, out of kindness, helps him from the room. This only places Lydgate in a worse light and he is aware of this. Mr Brooke and Mr Farebrother call on Dorothea to tell her what has happened. She refuses to believe that Lydgate is guilty.

COMMENTARY (Chapters 70–1): There are several points to be noticed in these two chapters. First of all there is George Eliot's sharp criticism of the people of Middlemarch. They attack their victims like a pack of hounds and reveal their conservatism, racism and anti-semitism, a subject she dealt with at length in another novel, *Daniel Deronda* (1876). She also indicates that the accusers are little better than the accused (see her epigraph to Chapter 85).

She is at pains to point out that Bulstrode is not a straightforward Dickensian hypocrite (a flat character) but is a far more complex figure. This is particularly important here, for it accounts for Lydgate's willingness to give Bulstrode the benefit of the doubt. Notice, too, how careful George Eliot has been to build up Lydgate's favourable view of Bulstrode. In Chapter 69 Lydgate had pondered on Bulstrode's care for Raffles and reached the conclusion that 'It is curious what patches of hardness and tenderness lie side by side in men's dispositions'. Because he has already been thinking along these lines it then 'appeared to him a very natural movement in Bulstrode that he should have reconsidered his refusal' (Chapter 70).

The two chapters also provide us with an instance of dramatic irony which at the same time reveals how carefully George Eliot builds her plots. Bulstrode believes himself safe from discovery because Raffles is in a town forty miles away (this also gives us an indication of the different attitudes to distances in our time and the time in which the novel was written). What Bulstrode did not take into account was that a horse-dealer—in this case Bambridge—would be likely to travel round the country to attend fairs and also likely to get into company with people like Raffles.

Finally it is a measure of Lydgate's humanity that he can feel compassion for Bulstrode, the man in many ways responsible for his present plight. Unlike most others, Lydgate is willing to give Bulstrode the benefit of the doubt. 'What we call the "just possible" is sometimes true and the thing we find it easier to believe is grossly false' (Chapter 73). Compare this attitude with that of the others excepting Dorothea.

NOTES AND GLOSSARY:
Botany Bay: a convict settlement in Australia
went over to the Romans: Arthur Wellesley, first Duke of Wellington (1769–1852), changed his view and eventually supported Catholic emancipation

BOOK EIGHT: SUNSET AND SUNRISE

Chapter 72

Dorothea, eager to clear Lydgate's name, suggests talking to him. The others, Sir James, Mr Brooke and Mr Farebrother, are opposed to this line of action and advise her to be cautious. Dorothea feels frustrated.

COMMENTARY: Dorothea's concern for Lydgate and her belief 'that people are almost always better than their neighbours think they are' stand out in sharp relief to the attitude displayed by the majority of the people in the previous chapter. Her attitude is also contrasted with Mr Farebrother's who advises caution. He does this for two reasons; first, because he knows how proud Lydgate is and how he would shrink from discussing his personal affairs, and, second, because his knowledge of human nature helps him to understand how certain circumstances may force even a man like Lydgate to stoop to deeds he would normally abhor. Dorothea in her naiveté takes neither of these things into account but the reader feels that George Eliot supports Dorothea's point of view and action rather than those of the others.

NOTES AND GLOSSARY:
Nemesis: retribution for one's sins

Chapter 73

Lydgate takes Bulstrode home and then rides several miles out of town to think matters over. He is bitter and depressed for, through no fault of his own, he sees his life in ruins. He determines to stay on in Middlemarch and in this small way demonstrate that he feels no guilt.

COMMENTARY: Shakespeare's lines 'There's a divinity that shapes our ends,/ Rough-hew them how we will' (*Hamlet* V.2.10-11) could well be the epigraph for this chapter. We are made to feel pity for the man who 'had meant everything to turn out differently'. There is an added sense of tragic loss when we think how a man, with noble intellect and purpose, is destroyed because of the whims and material greed of an unworthy wife. Lydgate, like Dorothea, is sometimes naïve but like her he also possesses nobility of character and is willing to think the best and not the worst of people. His human compassion overrides his natural dislike and he determines to stand by Bulstrode even though he knows that in the town's eyes this is further evidence of his guilt.

Chapter 74

The people of Middlemarch take malicious delight in the downfall of Bulstrode and those connected with him, particularly Lydgate and Rosamond. They do however feel pity for Mrs Bulstrode who remains ignorant of the facts. She realises that something is wrong and eventually her brother, Mr Vincy, tells her all. Heartbroken, she returns home and after some time, having removed all her finery, she goes to see her husband with the firm resolution that in spite of what has happened she will remain loyal to him.

COMMENTARY: 'On the whole, one might say that an ardent charity was at work setting the virtuous mind to make a neighbour unhappy for her good'. In this chapter George Eliot's sarcasm is directed at the people of Middlemarch, at their meanness and hypocrisy and their ghoulish delight in the misfortunes of others.

NOTES AND GLOSSARY:
methodistical: one who belonged to one of the Low churches, though not necessarily the Methodist church
fit for Newgate: Newgate was a famous prison in London
like an early Methodist: dressed in a very plain fashion

Chapter 75

Rosamond is a little happier after the creditors have been paid but she is still bored and wants Lydgate to move to London. She indulges in fantasies about Will Ladislaw who, she believes, must secretly love her—for she cannot conceive of any man preferring another woman to her. Unbeknown to Lydgate she sends out invitations to a dinner party. When all the invitations are refused she realises that something is wrong. She visits her parents and Mr Vincy tells her what has happened. On hearing the news the only pity she feels is for herself and she strengthens her resolve to make Lydgate move to London. She also decides to tell Will all about her problems when he comes.

COMMENTARY: In this chapter, as in the previous three, George Eliot shows us the reactions of various people to the misfortunes of others. Rosamond's lack of compassion for her husband is contrasted sharply with Mrs Bulstrode's loyalty to Mr Bulstrode, particularly when we consider that Bulstrode is guilty and his wife knows it.

Mr Bulstrode's desire to leave Middlemarch is more understandable and justifiable than Rosamond's. He leaves because of shame, she not so much because of shame but because she thinks that she will have a more pleasurable life in London.

On the positive side we have the loyalty, compassion, and courage of Dorothea, Lydgate and Mrs Bulstrode—on the negative side we have the selfishness of Rosamond, the maliciousness of the townspeople, and the cautionary reserve of people like Sir James and, to a certain degree, even Mr Farebrother.

Chapter 76

Dorothea asks Lydgate to come to see her. When he arrives she tells him that she believes in his innocence and asks him to tell her the facts as he knows them. Touched by her belief in him Lydgate does so and Dorothea promises to speak to her relatives and to Mr Farebrother. She proposes to take over the hospital and asks Lydgate to remain in charge. Lydgate tells her that this is not possible. His wife wishes to leave Middlemarch and he must give up his medical research and 'do as other men do, and think what will please the world and bring in money'. Dorothea is horrified at this prospect and suggests that she speak to Rosamond. Lydgate is grateful for this suggestion though doubtful that it will help.

When he leaves, Dorothea writes a cheque for £1,000 which she plans to take with her the next day when she visits Rosamond.

COMMENTARY: Dorothea and Lydgate are linked, a) because they both value the intellect more than material possessions, b) they both wish to serve mankind, c) they both made unfortunate marriages which gives them an understanding into one another's problems, d) they are willing to think the best and not the worst of people, e) they are willing to go against public opinion when they know that they are innocent—for example, Lydgate refuses to be driven out of Middlemarch, and Dorothea will eventually marry Will.

Chapter 77

Dorothea believes that Ladislaw loves her though she has no intention

of marrying him. She goes to visit Rosamond and the servant ushers
Dorothea into the drawing room unaware that Rosamond is there.
When she enters Dorothea finds Will there holding Rosamond's
hands, both looking intently at one another. She deposits the letter and
leaves immediately, convinced that Will and Rosamond are having an
affair. This makes her even more determined to clear Lydgate's name
and she spends the day trying to do so.

Chapter 78

Will realises what Dorothea must be thinking and rather irrationally
turns his fury on Rosamond. He accuses her of ruining his life and tells
her that he never contemplated any other woman than Dorothea.
Rosamond is completely taken aback by Will's outburst; her illusions
and her belief in her power over men are both shattered and when Will
leaves she collapses completely distraught on her bed. This is how
Lydgate finds her on his return. He immediately feels compassion for
her and we feel that, momentarily at least, she has some understanding
of how he has been hurt.

Chapter 79

Lydgate is unaware that Will was there in the morning. He thinks that
it is Dorothea's visit that has upset Rosamond and is surprised when
Will turns up in the evening. Lydgate tells Will what has happened and
that the town knows of Will's connection with Bulstrode and Raffles.
This embitters Will even further for he believes that it will give
Dorothea yet another reason to despise him.

Chapter 80

In order to forget her sorrow and upset, Dorothea has been active all
day. She continues in this rather over-animated fashion during the
dinner that evening at the Farebrothers but when Will's name comes
up she is no longer able to control her feelings and returns home. On
arriving there she flings herself to the floor and cries herself to sleep.
The next morning she wakes up determined to forget Will and to lead
an active and full life by helping the poor. To indicate this she discards
her mourning clothes. She then resolves to visit Rosamond once more
as she feels that Lydgate is the person most in need of help.

NOTES AND GLOSSARY:

all of a mummy: a pulpy substance

White of Selbourne: Gilbert White (1720–93) wrote about the birds,
animals and plants of the village of Selbourne

a mother . . . by the sword: refers to Solomon's judgement in the Bible,
   I Kings 3: 16-28
mater dolorosa: name given to a painting which depicts Mary
                     sorrowing for Christ

Chapter 81

Dorothea goes to visit Rosamond. Lydgate greets her and tells her he
accepts her cheque. Rosamond is a little frightened about meeting
Dorothea but she is soon reassured as Dorothea speaks gently to her
about Lydgate and about the need for love and trust in marriage and
the destructiveness of illicit affairs. Rosamond, overcome by
Dorothea's kindness and understanding, tells Dorothea that it is
Dorothea that Will loves and not her. Dorothea is overjoyed though
she can hardly comprehend what Rosamond is telling her. Soon after,
she departs, leaving Rosamond and Lydgate together, not happy but
less unhappy than before.

COMMENTARY: For once Rosamond's action is not a selfish one, though
we feel it is still partly motivated by her desire to vindicate herself in
Will's eyes. Rosamond's response is also due to Dorothea's behaviour,
'the saving influence of a noble nature'.

Chapter 82

Will, seeking an excuse to visit Middlemarch, had decided to ask
Bulstrode for the money that is rightfully his, so as to finance a
settlement in the Far West. After Dorothea's unexpected entrance
into the drawing room at Lydgate's he feels like leaving Middlemarch
again. However, he decides to stay and to visit the Lydgates.
Rosamond lets him know that she has told Dorothea the truth. Will
still fears that Dorothea might hold the incident against him.

NOTES AND GLOSSARY:
The Rubicon: a small stream in Italy. In 48BC the Roman general
                     Julius Caesar led his army across it, thereby
                     declaring war on Pompey. The phrase 'to cross the
                     Rubicon' means to take an irrevocable step

---

Chapter 83

Will comes once more to say goodbye to Dorothea. As a storm rages
outside they confess their love for one another. Will, having pointed
out how hopeless it all is because of his poverty, is on the point of
departure when Dorothea breaks down, and declares that she does not

care about money and that they have enough to live on.

COMMENTARY: Dorothea's final words in this chapter show another instance of the contrast between her and Rosamond.

NOTES AND GLOSSARY:

had flannel: one way of being charitable was to distribute flannel to the poor

---

Chapter 84

Mr Brooke announces that Dorothea intends to marry Will. Everyone is surprised and Sir James is furious, partly because he despises Will, and partly because he had hoped that the Tipton and Freshitt estates would eventually go to his son. He declares that he will never speak to Dorothea again. Celia drives over to Dorothea to try to persuade her to change her mind but Dorothea is determined to marry Will.

COMMENTARY: This chapter provides an excellent example of George Eliot's ability to poke gentle fun at some of her characters and to reveal their weaknesses without savaging them. Celia's inclination towards pretension and status is satirised gently in her wishing for her husband to be an Earl, as then her son would be a viscount, and thinking of 'his lordship's little tooth coming through'. She may be complacent and even a little naïve about everyday life—'How can you always live in a street'—but she still knows her sister; 'Dodo never minded about precedence if she could have her own way'.

Mr and Mrs Cadwallader's different natures are revealed in the way each of them suggests that Sir James's upset about Dorothea marrying may have a certain degree of self-interest in it.

NOTES AND GLOSSARY:

a Draco, a Jeffreys: Draco, when Archon in Athens in 621BC, reorganised the laws with impartiality. His code was severe in the extreme, death being the penalty for almost every offence. Judge Jeffreys (1648–89) was notorious for brutality as a judge; he was known as the 'infamous Jeffreys', and during the 'bloody assize' after the Duke of Monmouth's rebellion he had hundreds of his followers fined, whipped, transported or hanged

---

Chapter 85

Mr Bulstrode is making preparations to leave Middlemarch. Anxious to please his wife, who is suffering terribly, he asks her if there is anything he can do. She suggests helping Rosamond and Lydgate but Bulstrode tells her that he thinks Lydgate would refuse such help. However, as an alternative he proposes that Fred Vincy should become manager of Stone Court under the direction of Caleb Garth.

COMMENTARY: George Eliot once again reveals a degree of understanding and compassion for Bulstrode.

Chapter 86

Caleb speaks to Mary and asks her if she still wishes to marry Fred. When she says she does Caleb tells her about Stone Court. Shortly afterwards Fred arrives, Mary tells him the good news and they agree to marry.

Finale

Although Fred never becomes rich he gains the respect of the town and he and Mary live a life of happiness together with their three sons.

Lydgate builds up a successful practice in London but always considers himself a failure. Rosamond remains faithful to him but does not change her ways and when Lydgate dies at fifty she marries an older, wealthy physician.

Dorothea never regrets marrying Will who is eventually elected to Parliament. When their first son is born a reconciliation takes place between them and Sir James, though Ladislaw and Sir James never really like one another.

Mr Brooke does not break the entail which means that after his death his property goes to Dorothea's son.

COMMENTARY: 'Who can quit young lives after being long in company with them, and not desire to know what befell them in their after-years?'

George Eliot follows the literary conventions of the day by telling her readers what lay ahead for her characters.

NOTES AND GLOSSARY:

Municipal Reform: refers to the English Municipal Corporations Reform Act which was passed in 1835

a river of which Cyrus broke the strength: the river is the Gyndes which Cyrus the Great of Persia divided into many channels because it barred his progress

Part 3

Commentary

The social, economic, religious and political background

The events in *Middlemarch* take place during a clearly defined period, namely from 30 September 1829 to the end of May 1832, a period just prior to the passing of the Reform Act of 1832. In the first part of this period the Tory, anti-Reform forces were in power; mention is made in Chapter 3 of 'those anti-reform times'. With the death of George IV in June 1830 the Whigs, under Lord Grey, gained control and finally in June 1832 the First Reform Bill was passed.

This section will examine the circumstances and events which led to the passing of the Reform Bill. By 1815 the process known as 'enclosures' had in effect been completed. Wealthy and powerful landowners were able, because they controlled parliament, to pass legislation which enabled them to enclose the open fields which by tradition had been for everybody's use. It is true that in many cases the open-field system was wasteful and that the enclosure of the land led to much improved agricultural methods, with a high increase in productivity, and as a consequence, a much higher income for the already wealthy landowner. When the price of corn fell after the Napoleonic wars the landowners introduced the Corn Laws which prohibited the import of foreign corn until the price of corn in the home market had reached 80 shillings a quarter. This ensured the continued wealth of the landowners whilst, at the same time, it increased the hardship of everyone else in the country. What it also did was create a split between the landed interests and the manufacturing interests, with the former favouring monopoly and the latter free trade.

It was not the manufacturers, however, who suffered most. For if enclosures meant added property and increased wealth for the already wealthy landowners it meant dispossession and poverty for those who had formerly farmed the 'common' land. Some became tenant farmers at the mercy of the landowners, some of whom were progressive like Sir James Chettam, while others were like Mr Brooke, who refused to spend any money on improvement and who justly deserved the anger of tenants like Dagley (see Chapter 39). Other dispossessed farmers became agricultural labourers who lived in abject poverty and sometimes, as a protest against the conditions, burnt hay and corn-ricks (see Chapter 3). Thomson tells of a group of starving field labourers who in 1830 rioted in support of their demand for a wage of half-a-crown a day. Three of them were hanged and four hundred and twenty were deported to Australia*. Some labourers also turned to poaching (stealing game) from the rich landowners' properties but, if they were caught, the penalty was severe, for the Game Laws, like the Corn Laws, were there to protect the interests of the rich. Only the squire— or the squire's eldest son—was allowed to kill game. The ordinary man if caught poaching a hare or a rabbit could be transported to Australia for seven years. (See for example the fate of Bunch, the sheep stealer, in Chapter 4.

In those times little connection was made between crime and poverty; the law existed essentially to protect the interests and property of the rich. There were some two hundred and twenty crimes that carried the death penalty, many of them minor offences, for example, stealing five shillings from a shop. The death sentence was sometimes commuted to transportation for life to Botany Bay. This British settlement in New South Wales was primarily founded because of the need to find a suitable place for the so-called criminal population. Australia was deemed ideal as it was a place 'that provided little facility for return'!

Another alternative offered to the landless agricultural labourers was to drift to the new towns which were emerging because of the industrial revolution; towns such as Manchester, Birmingham and Coventry (Middlemarch is the fictional name for Coventry). Here they worked under appalling conditions in the mills, factories and mines.

If enclosures created hardships for the agricultural labourers the new machines created equal hardships for the village handloom weavers, for they were no longer able to compete with the machines. As a protest they at times attempted to smash the machines (see Mr Brooke's reference to 'machine-breaking' in Chapter 3). There is also a reference in Chapter 34 to Mr Vincy's exploitation of the handloom weavers of Tipton and Freshitt. Admittedly it is Mrs Cadwallader who makes the remark, and she despises Mr Vincy because of his lower social status, but it is also likely that Mr Vincy is able to exploit the weavers because he knows they cannot compete with the machines.

The industrial revolution was to change Britain from an agricultural country into an industrial nation. In 1815 most Englishmen worked on the land; by 1830 it is estimated that half the population lived under urban conditions. If the industrial revolution created untold misery for the many it also created untold wealth for the few, the industrialists. By doing so it changed the social structure of the country.

*David Thomson, *England in the Nineteenth Century (1815–1914)*, Penguin Books, Harmondsworth, 1955, pp.16-17.

It was not surprising that the new industrialists should seek political power commensurate with their new found wealth by gaining representation in Parliament for the new industrial towns of the Midlands and the North. They set about wresting the power from the landed gentry who controlled parliament by abolishing rotten boroughs. (A rotten borough was also called a pocket borough; this was a town which had dwindled in importance, had very few voters and yet was represented in parliament; Hawley and Hackbutt discuss rotten boroughs in Chapter 37.)

Another point on which the two power groups were to differ was that of monopoly and free trade. The landed gentry and the plantation owners (absentee landlords whose estates were in the Caribbean and who held many of the rotten boroughs) were in favour of monopoly; the commercial interests wanted free trade. Free trade is the cry of the man who fears no competition, and at that point in history Britain had no industrial rival. The problem was that reform and changes in policy could only be brought about by parliament. How did one reform a parliament that was controlled by the anti-reform group? The difference in interests was to lead to an open rift between the landed gentry and the new merchant and commercial classes.

In *Middlemarch* the landed gentry are represented by Sir James Chettam, Mr Brooke and Mrs Cadwallader; the new merchant classes by Mr Vincy, Mr Bulstrode and other wealthy citizens of Middlemarch. It becomes very obvious to a reader of the novel that the former group despises the latter and that they regard money as less important than birth. This is exemplified in Mrs Cadwallader, who is a snob. By marrying Mr Cadwallader she has married beneath her in both rank and wealth. However, this does not matter because her own genteel birth assures her a place in the society into which she was born. She considers farmers without masters to be 'monsters', 'as curious' to her 'as any buffaloes or bisons' (Chapter 34). The group from Freshitt and Tipton look down both literally and metaphorically on the other group who are attending Peter Featherstone's funeral (Chapter 34).

Mr Brooke may invite the male citizens of Middlemarch to his dinner party but he is careful not to invite their wives. It may be all right for the men of the two worlds to meet, indeed it was becoming more and more expedient, but the women are not to be tainted by contact. Something of the same idea can be found in some multi-racial societies today where the white community may allow their sons to play with coloured children but never their daughters. Lydgate is anxious to let it be known that he comes of a good family, and Rosamond is equally anxious to marry him because of that. In other words, we find no resentment on the part of the middle classes against Mrs Cadwallader's group. Their aim is not to destroy the other group but to join it; for example, the Vincys have social aspirations for Fred and are disappointed when he fails to fulfil them.

The arrogance and snobbery of the landed gentry provided George Eliot with plenty of opportunities to be ironical at their expense. Perhaps the best instance of this occurs in Chapter 84. When Mr Brooke appears with a glum face the rest of the group think it is because the Reform Bill has been rejected by the Lords and they show little concern for his dejection. However, when he tells them the real cause for his concern, they are horrified at the prospect of one of 'them' marrying someone outside their group and a part foreigner into the bargain. Through their disproportionate concern George Eliot stresses how small the world of the landed gentry is, how complacent they are about their own position and how ignorant they are of events that will have such far-reaching effects on their lives as well as on many others.

Critics have wondered why George Eliot chose to link what in the first place were two separate novels. Several suggestions have been offered; the time and setting were the same, there was also the similarity between the characters of Dorothea and Lydgate. What could also be a reason is that looking back on events that took place forty years earlier George Eliot could see the beginning of a movement that was to make radical changes in all sections of English society.

Religion and the Catholic question

Whilst the Toleration Act of 1689 had given the Protestant dissenters (those Protestants who were not Anglicans) a certain degree of religious freedom it had not extended this freedom to Roman Catholics. The latter were excluded from ministerial or administrative office, from commissions in the armed services and from the universities. Not only was there official discrimination against them, there was also popular prejudice.

The rapid rise in the number of Protestant dissenters plus their increasing wealth led to growing pressure to repeal the Test and Corporation Acts of Charles II that discriminated against non-Anglicans and so break the Anglican monopoly on public office. The dissenters' cause was taken up by several Whig leaders, among them Lord John Russell, who in 1829 managed to get a bill through parliament which repealed the Test and Corporation Acts. The bill however did not apply to Catholics and the struggle for Catholic emancipation was to be a bitter one.

What eventually led to reform was not agitation by the English Catholics, who were only a very small percentage of the population, but agitation by the Catholics in Ireland who represented the vast majority of the population there but who had no right to vote or to sit in parliament because of their religion. In 1828 the voters of County Clare elected Daniel O'Connell, even though, as a Catholic, he was forbidden to take up his seat. The British government feared that other constituencies would do the same and that civil war would ensue. Rather than face such a danger, despite their previous opposition to Catholic emancipation, the Tory government, under the leadership of the Duke of Wellington and with Sir Robert Peel as Home Secretary, passed the Roman Catholic Relief Act of 1829, an Act which placed Catholics on the same civil footing as the Protestant dissenters. Wellington's and Peel's change of policy explains such remarks in *Middlemarch* as 'Wellington and Peel generally depreciated' (Chapter 37), or 'when [Wellington] turned his coat and went over to the Romans' (Chapter 71).

The followers of the established church, that is, the Church of England, belonged to the aristocracy, the landed gentry and the rural population. As a man moved up the social scale through a betterment of his financial situation it was possible he might change from being a dissenter or non-conformist to becoming a member of the established church, as in the case of Mr Bulstrode. The Protestant churches found their followers essentially among the new rising middle classes, the merchants and bankers in the City, the manufacturers in the new industrial towns and the poorer section of the urban population. (For an account of the link and relationship between dissenters, puritanism and capitalism see R. H. Tawney, *Religion and the Rise of Capitalism*, Penguin Books, Harmondsworth, 1969.)

Politics and the political system before reform

There were two major political parties, the Tories and the Whigs. The Tories were conservative, opposed to reform and in favour of a hierarchy both of Church and State. Needless to say their supporters belonged to the Church of England, the aristocracy and the landed gentry. The supporters of the Whig party came mainly from the Protestant dissenters, the City bankers and the new rising merchant and manufacturing interests. It is not surprising therefore that this party tried to wrest some of the power from the landed interests and distribute it more equally among the new and powerful classes. In view of this, it is easy to see why the people at Freshitt and Tipton thought Mr Brooke a traitor to his class.

Whilst the Whig party was in favour of reform it was not in favour of universal suffrage (this did not take place in England until 1928). Both parties believed that property not people should be represented in Parliament. Unlike the Radicals, the Whigs were not interested in a parliamentary reform that would give rights to the masses; they were only interested in ensuring that those who possessed wealth through industry and commerce could take their place alongside the landed property owners in the running of the country. The shift of wealth, power and population from the country to the industrial towns had made the privileges of the landed interests an anomaly. The Whig party and its followers were determined to rectify this anomaly. The doctrine of inherited privileges was challenged by that of the survival of the fittest.

The same period saw the rise of the railways (*Middlemarch*, Chapter 56) and they too were to play a role in reform by making the people who lived in the new industrial towns aware of how unjust the parliamentary voting system was. Thomson quotes a Manchester man who commented on the opening of the new Manchester and Liverpool railway in September 1830. The man wrote:

> Parliamentary Reform must follow soon after the opening of this road. A million of persons will pass over it in the course of this year, and see that hitherto unseen village of Newton; and they must be convinced of the absurdity of its sending two members to Parliament, whilst Manchester sends none.*

Eventually the forces of Reform won. Lord John Russell's Reform Bill was rejected at first by the House of Lords (see Chapter 84) but a short while later the Lords were forced to give in and the Bill that was to have such far-reaching effects became law.

The actual Reform Bill of 1832 was very conservative according to present-day British standards. It did extend the franchise but in a very limited and, at times, negative way. For example one group to whom the franchise was extended was the fifty-pounds tenants-at-will, a group that was to prove a very vulnerable section of the country electorate, open to bribery and corruption (see Chapters 37–8 in *Middlemarch*, in particular Chapter 38 where we are told that Giles 'spent ten thousand pounds and failed because he did not bribe enough').

What was more important was the redistribution of seats among the constituencies. Fifty-six rotten boroughs were abolished, thirty others had their representation reduced from two to one member whilst forty-two new constituences were given representation and for the most part these were the new industrial towns like Manchester, Birmingham and Leeds.

Middlemarch abounds with historical events but at no time does one feel one is reading a social or historical treatise instead of a work of

---

*David Thomson, *England in the Nineteenth Century (1815–1914)*, Penguin Books, Harmondsworth, 1955, p.42.

fiction. George Eliot presents us with history but never obtrusively. What she does is to present it 'dramatically, within the story, as part of the lives of her characters'.*

The origin and composition of *Middlemarch*

Thanks to the existence of George Eliot's letters and journals as well as of the manuscript and the notebook† she kept when writing *Middlemarch* we are able to form a very accurate idea of the origin and composition of her novel. These documents also help us to gain an insight into her creative method. Jerome Beaty has done extensive research into this aspect of *Middlemarch* in his book *'Middlemarch' from Notebook to Novel***.

The novel as we know it today was not how George Eliot originally conceived it: in the beginning it was to be not one novel but two. We know from her letters that about New Year's Day 1869 George Eliot decided to write a novel to be called 'Middlemarch'††, we know that it was to be a novel about provincial life and that the hero was to be a physician. We know also from the letters that by 11 September, 1869 she had completed an introduction and three chapters and that by May 1870 she had written some more, though as she told her publisher John Blackwood, she was 'not so far along as she intended to be'. In November 1870 George Eliot began another story. Her journal entry for 2 December 1870 reads:

> I am experimenting in a story which I began without any serious intention of carrying it out lengthily. It is a subject which has been recorded among my possible themes ever since I began to write fiction, but will probably take new shapes in the development. I am today at p.44.

Her journal entry for 31 December 1870 reads:

> I have written only 100 pages—good printed pages—of a story which I began about the opening of November, and at present mean to call 'Miss Brooke'.

*Jerome Beaty, 'History by Indirection: the Era of Reform in *Middlemarch*' in *Victorian Studies*, 1,2, December, 1957, p.175.
†Anna Theresa Kitchel (ed.), *George Eliot's Quarry for 'Middlemarch'*, University of California Press, 1950. Anna Kitchel has edited George Eliot's notebook which the latter called 'Quarry for Middlemarch'. The notebook was a small, black leather notebook, 4 by 6½ inches. Half of the book is devoted principally to notes on scientific, particularly medical writers, plus political dates. The book is then turned over and the other half used chiefly for working out the structure of the novel.
**Jerome Beaty, *'Middlemarch' from Notebook to Novel*, University of Illinois Press, Urbana, 1960.
††As in Beaty, the title of the earlier 'Middlemarch' is put in quotation marks, and the title of the published *Middlemarch*, the novel as we know it today, is italicised.

The next significant journal entry in connection with *Middlemarch* occurs on 19 March 1871:

> I have written about 236 pages (print) of my Novel, which I want to get off my hands by next November. My present fear is that I have too much matter, to many '*momenti*'.

With the evidence that we have it can be stated with relative certainty that the novel George Eliot refers to is *Middlemarch* as we know it, that by that date George Eliot had written the first eighteen chapters of *Middlemarch* plus what is now Chapter 23 and that these chapters consisted of a fusion of the original 'Middlemarch' story with the 'Miss Brooke' story as well as some material that would link the two stories. Evidence also leads us to believe that the first nine and a half chapters or ninety-six pages belonged to the 'Miss Brooke' story, which in the manuscript ended on page 96 midway through the present Chapter 10. The next sixteen pages of manuscript have been established as bridging pages written to link the two stories; the dinner party scene in Chapter 10 links 'Middlemarch' with 'Miss Brooke' by introducing 'Middlemarch' characters into the world of Miss Brooke. What follows these bridging pages is without doubt the hundred or more pages George Eliot had written of 'Middlemarch' though not necessarily in their original version or order—for example, the present Chapter 15 is likely to have been the original Introduction. What George Eliot did was to rewrite these pages to fit them into the new *Middlemarch*. There is no evidence that any of the chapters after Chapter 16 were written as part of 'Middlemarch' or 'Miss Brooke' whilst, from Chapter 18 on, the two worlds and two stories become more and more interrelated.

Another factor, which was to ensure that in the remainder of the book the two worlds would be interrelated, was the method of publication. In those days as today, economic considerations entered into the publishing world. George Eliot had early on expressed the fear that she had 'too many *momenti*' (Journal entry, 19 March 1871). As she continued to write, her fears were confirmed and it became obvious that there would be more material than could fit even the three-volume format of her previous novel, *Felix Holt*. John Blackwood, her publisher, had lost a considerable amount of money on *Felix Holt*, and would therefore be rather unwilling to risk a four-volume work. It was George Eliot's husband G. H. Lewes who came up with a solution:

> Mrs Lewes finds that she will require 4 volumes for her story, not 3. I winced at the idea at first, but the story must not be spoiled for want of space, and as you have more than once spoken of the desirability of inventing some mode of circumventing the Libraries and making

the public *buy* in stead of borrowing I have devised the following scheme, suggested by the plan Victor Hugo followed with his long *Misérables*—namely to publish it in *half-volume parts* either at intervals of one, or as I think better, two months. The eight parts at 5/- could yield the £2 for the four volumes, and at two month intervals would not be dearer than *Maga*. Each part would have a certain unity and completeness in itself with separate title. Thus the work is called *Middlemarch*. Part I will be *Miss Brooke*.

Blackwood agreed and *Middlemarch* was published in eight half-volume parts at two-monthly intervals with the exception of the last three parts which were issued monthly. The first half-volume was published in December 1871 and the last in December 1872.

How much did publication in parts, considered by many to be detrimental to the organic unity of a book, affect *Middlemarch*? It has been argued, probably quite rightly, that it had no negative effect on the novel. The half-volume requirement gave George Eliot much more flexibility than that small monthly-parts form used by Thackeray and Dickens for *Vanity Fair* and *David Copperfield*. She was never faced with the dilemma that Dickens experienced in writing *David Copperfield*. John Butt tells us that:

> When the proofs of Part III reached him, Dickens found that he had overstepped his monthly allowance of thirty-two pages by thirty-five lines of type. Something had to be sacrificed, and this [description of David's mother's funeral] was one of the passages cut. It involves a small but appreciable relaxing of the tension.*

She was however very conscious of her readership and of the need for each half-volume to 'look' the right size, as the correspondence between Lewes and Blackwood bears out. All are concerned about the 'thickness' of the book. In his letter to Blackwood of 7 September 1871 Lewes writes:

> By the way a thought strikes me. Would it not be well to have an advertisement sheet bound up with each part—as Dickens & Thackeray had with their parts? (though not of course on the *covers*). This would not only bring in some hard cash, it would help make the volume look bigger for the 5/- which in British eyes is a consideration not to be neglected.

Lewes brings up the question again in his letter of 11 September. 'The book' he says, 'must *not look* thin for 5/-'. Blackwood reassures Lewes. In his letter of 25 February 1872 he tells him first of all that it is quality not quantity that counts: 'Do not disturb yourself about Book III being

---

*John Butt, 'The composition of *David Copperfield* (I)' in *The Dickensian*, 46 (Spring, 1950), p.94.

thin—there is the matter of volumes in it'. What is more Blackwood, a canny Scotsman, had found a solution to the problem. The letter continues, 'Besides the acute Simpson is using paper for the part which will make it bulk about the same as the others'.

What mattered more than the length of each part was the need for each book to be complete in itself; each part was to have 'a certain unity & completeness in itself', and yet at the same time lead naturally into the next book. In his letter to Blackwood of 7 September 1871, Lewes showed himself conscious of this need:

> We have added on to the end of part I that portion of part II which closes with the scene at the miserly uncle's (chaps. 11 and 12)—a capital bit to end with; and this new arrangement not only pitches the interest forward into part II & prepares the way for the people & for Dodo's absence from part II, but also equalizes quantities better, though making part I rather longer than II which however is desirable.

There can be little doubt that from Book Three onwards George Eliot wrote with all these considerations in mind, and so it can be argued that publication in parts, rather than destroying the structure and unity of the novel, was a constructive element in achieving the inter-relationship and interdependence of plot and characters for which *Middlemarch* is so justly famous.

Structure

Structure is a term used for the organisation of overall design. It comprises all the aspects that go into the making of the work—for instance, character, events, setting, outside and inside forces and influences. The more successful the integration and interaction of these elements, the more successful the work of art.

Closely related to structure is plot. Plot is the organisation of events in the work. A unified plot, such as we find in classical Greek drama, is one in which every incident has a role to play and no incident can be left out without destroying the 'structure'. Contrasted with the unified plot is the episodic plot in which the incidents are loosely connected or may even have no connection whatsoever.

George Eliot stands out among her contemporary novelists for her structural craftsmanship. Lord David Cecil comments on this: 'It is very rare for a Victorian novelist before George Eliot to conceive the story as an organic whole of which every incident and character forms a contributory and integral part.'*

*Lord David Cecil, *Early Victorian Novelists*, Constable, London, 1934, p. 230

Nowhere is George Eliot's craftsmanship in creating a unified structure more in evidence than in *Middlemarch*. When it was first published the critic for the *Saturday Review* commented on its structural integrity and wrote: 'Each chapter of the story has been written with every other chapter in view, each fitting into each as exactly as the pieces in some elaborate Chinese puzzle.'*

When we consider her vast cast, of nearly one hundred and fifty people, the fact that she is dealing with not just one plot or even two but at least four, a) Dorothea-Casaubon-Ladislaw, b) Lydgate-Rosamond, c) Mary-Fred, d) Bulstrode-Ladislaw-Raffles, and that she succeeds in successfully interweaving and interrelating these plots and is able to hold our attention for over nine hundred pages, we cannot but wonder at her achievement. She is careful to account for the smallest detail; each incident proceeds logically out of an earlier one; and each and every one of the structural elements interacts with the others to produce 'complete organism'.

There are coincidences but these never exceed the bounds of probability. Each event is carefully prepared for, sometimes hundreds of pages before it happens, but when it does happen we recognise that it is a logical consequence of all that has gone before; for example, think of the far-reaching effects of Raffles' picking up the piece of paper at Stone Court. (See also the commentary on Chapters 70-71 on the choice of Mr Bambridge's occupation.) The same attention to detail and logical consistency is to be found in her characters' reaction to events and to other characters. When seeming inconsistencies occur, if we look carefully, we shall see that George Eliot has prepared the way. This is particularly noticeable in connection with Lydgate and Bulstrode (see commentary on Chapters 70-71).

George Eliot herself commented on the question of improbability in a letter to her publisher:

> My stories always grow out of psychological conception of dramatis personae . . . I cannot stir a step aside from what I *feel* to be *true* in character. If anything strikes you as untrue to human nature in my delineations, I shall be very glad if you will point it out to me, that I may reconsider the matter. But alas! inconsistencies and weaknesses are not untrue.†

What else contributes to the structural unity of *Middlemarch*? There is of course throughout the entire novel the controlling presence of George Eliot herself in the role of omniscient author. The use of the word 'controlling' is not meant to suggest that we or the characters are

*_Saturday Review_, 7 December 1872.
†Letter to John Blackwood in *The George Eliot Letters*, ed. Gordon S. Haight, Yale University Press, New Haven, 1954, Vol. II, p. 297.

puppets to be manipulated. On the contrary. (See the section 'Authorial intrusion and the question of compassion' below, for comment on this.)

In each book George Eliot very carefully paves the way for events to come and also successfully accounts for the absence of a certain character or characters from the scene for a period of time (see, for example, Dorothea's departure to Rome for her honeymoon). She is equally careful to have a large social scene in most of the books, where some characters from each of the main plots come together, for example, Mr Brooke's dinner party or Peter Featherstone's funeral.

Another way of achieving structural unity is the use of comparisons and contrasts, both in the plots themselves and in the characters. When Mrs Bulstrode reacts in the way she does to Mr Bulstrode's misfortune we cannot help remembering Rosamond's attitude to Lydgate. Or when Lydgate bemoans his own fate, 'Only those who know the supremacy of the intellectual life . . . can understand the grief of one who falls from that serene activity into the absorbing soul-wasting struggle with worldly annoyances' (Chapter 73), the reader immediately thinks of Dorothea. Such contrasts and parallels exist throughout the novel and create resonances that lead the readers to reach far beyond the particular incident to an all-inclusive view of human nature. Henry James, himself a great novelist, wrote about *Middlemarch*:

> Each plot [the histories of Lydgate and Dorothea] is a tale of matrimonial infelicity, but the conditions in each are so different and the circumstances so broadly opposed that the mind passes from one to the other with that supreme sense of the vastness and variety of human life, under aspects apparently similar, which it belongs only to the great novels to produce.*

Authorial intrusion and the question of compassion

One of the features that most strike the reader of *Middlemarch* today is the constant and obvious presence of the author in the novel. George Eliot makes no attempt to hide the fact that she is the omniscient author; again and again she breaks the narrative flow to step directly into the novel and formulate some generalisation which she wishes us to consider. This technique, known as authorial intrusion, was much used by other Victorian novelists; in *Middlemarch*, George Eliot

*Henry James, 'George Eliot's *Middlemarch*' in *A Century of George Eliot Criticism*, edited Gordon S. Haight, Methuen, London, 1966, p. 84.

actually comments on Fielding's use of it and regrets the passing of his conversations with the reader. It was, however, a technique that fell into disfavour in the twentieth century; the great innovators of technique in the novel, James Joyce and Virginia Woolf, abandoned it, and George Steiner, a modern critic, regards it as inept personal interference in the action. Even W. J. Harvey, one of the critics most sympathetic to George Eliot, has minimised the role of the remarks we find so frequently in her novels. 'They are,' he said, 'bridges between our world and the world of the novel. They are not ends in themselves, not the proper objects of contemplation. And we are meant to pass easily and quickly over these comments, these bridges.'*

Several well-known critics have objected to this criticism, including Isabel Armstrong who prefers to substitute the terms 'sayings' or 'wisdom' for 'authorial intrusion'.† Her argument is that they create 'bridges not between our world and the world of the novel', as Harvey suggested, 'but between the world of the novel and our world'. By moving 'between the known, the common experience', which is shared by the writer and reader alike, to 'the unknown, the unique and particular predicament of the novel',‡ these passages play a crucial role in creating the understanding and compassion that George Eliot demands of her readers. Sometimes the particular predicament comes first, to be followed by the generalisation, at other times the order is reversed. In support of her argument, Isabel Armstrong quotes the paragraph concerning Bulstrode which begins 'The spiritual kind of rescue was a genuine need with him' and concludes

> If this be hypocrisy, it is a process which shows itself occasionally in us all, to whatever confession we belong, and whether we believe in the future perfection of our race or in the nearest date fixed for the end of the world; whether we regard the earth as a putrefying nidus for a saved remnant, including ourselves, or have a passionate belief in the solidarity of mankind. (Chapter 61)

The movement, in ever widening circles from the singular person to the plural pronoun and finally to all mankind, is there to remind us that each and every one of us is vulnerable and capable of succumbing to the temptation to which Bulstrode succumbed. George Eliot goes to particular pains to involve us in this way when there may be a chance that we would dissociate outselves from the character and his predicament. This applies particularly to Bulstrode and Mr Casaubon.

*W. J. Harvey, *The Art of George Eliot*, Constable, London, 1961, p. 81.
†Isabel Armstrong, '*Middlemarch*: A Note on George Eliot's Wisdom' in *Critical Essays on George Eliot,* ed. Barbara Hardy, Routledge and Kegan Paul, London, 1970. See also Barbara Hardy, '*Middlemarch* and the Passions' in *This Particular Web*, ed. Ian Adam, University of Toronto Press, 1975.
‡Isabel Armstrong, op. cit., p. 121.

One of the most perfect illustrations of this technique is to be found in Chapter 42 where Mr Casaubon learns from Lydgate that there is a possibility he could die at any moment. The whole chapter seesaws between the statement of general, moral and psychological truths shared by us all and the presentation of the particular situation and feelings of one human being, Mr Casaubon.

The first thing we are told is that Mr Casaubon shrinks from pity. George Eliot then proceeds to build up the chapter in such a way that at the finish the one emotion we are incapable of withholding is our pity. This is not achieved by presenting Mr Casaubon as other than he is. The warts are there for us all to see. Nor does George Eliot sentimentalise him. The usual note of irony creeps in when the male/female relationship is discussed. Mr Casaubon regards the change in Dorothea from a 'young creature who had worshipped him . . . into the critical wife' as a betrayal. We quickly realise that George Eliot does not regard it in quite the same light. Mr Casaubon fears that he is no longer adored without criticism. George Eliot responds to this fear by asking the reader if Mr Casaubon has not got good reason for his suspicion. We detect the note of wry humour and cannot refrain from smiling at the very notion of Mr Casaubon and adorableness being linked. At this stage, George Eliot has isolated Mr Casaubon and his dilemma from us—we are mere spectators looking at a disagreeable and somewhat ridiculous man. Then, with a swift movement and by the use of a generalisation, she suddenly makes what seems to be a very foolish and impossible desire on his part appear to be the most natural thing in the world: it may be a foolish wish, but, she asks, is there anyone of us who would not wish for just one person who found us 'unmixedly adorable'? (Chapter 42).

Again and again she uses this method to increase our understanding and compassion. She asks us to realise that each life has many facets, that ambiguities and moral contradictions exist within each and every one of us, and, before we pass judgement on others, we should ask ourselves what our own reaction would have been in similar circumstances.

In *Middlemarch*, George Eliot presents us with a group of complex human beings, trapped sometimes by their own failings, sometimes through circumstances, and sometimes through a combination of both. None of them is completely innocent, not even those of whom George Eliot most obviously approves and whom she holds up for our admiration and sympathy, for example, Dorothea and Lydgate. Nor are any completely bad. Both Casaubon and Bulstrode are presented as negative characters, the latter more so than the former, but in the moment of crisis George Eliot asks for our understanding and even our sympathy, and it is a tribute to her genius that we are willing to give them. Bulstrode is a hypocrite, he has cheated Will of his inheritance and throughout the novel he has generally acted in a despicable manner. 'But this,' as George Eliot says of Mr Casaubon, 'is a very bare and therefore a very incomplete way of putting the case. The human soul moves in many channels' (Chapter 42). George Eliot is at pains to point out that Mr Bulstrode is not the simple hyopocrite that some would make him out; she succeeds in her efforts so that at the finish it is impossible to withhold our compassion from 'this unhappy man, who had longed for years to be better than he was' (Chapter 70).

Throughout the novel she is consantly setting us 'The difficult task of knowing another soul' (Chapter 12) in the hope that with knowledge might come understanding. She believed that Art for her had a moral mission, and in a letter to Charles Bray she wrote:

> If Art does not enlarge men's sympathies, it does nothing morally . . . the only effect I ardently long to produce by my writings, is that those who read them should be better able to *imagine* and to *feel* the pains and the joys of those who differ from themselves in everything but the broad fact of being struggling erring human creatures.*

George Eliot may often be ironical at the expense of her characters, even those with whom she obviously sympathises, for example, Dorothea or Lydgate, but she rarely fails to tinge the irony with a degree of compassion. One notable exception to this is her attitude towards the people who turn like a savage pack on Bulstrode and to a lesser extent on Lydgate. She is saying that to those who extend no compassion, none can be extended.

Feminist issues in *Middlemarch*

Middlemarch gives a very clear picture of the role and function of middle- and upper-class women in nineteenth-century England. It becomes immediately obvious that the woman is inferior in every way to the man and that the function of the wife is that described in the words of the marriage ceremony: 'to love, honour and obey', with emphasis on obedience. 'A woman dictates before marriage in order that she might have an appetite for submission afterwards' (Chapter 9). The woman's role was to serve her husband, to entertain him, to adorn his house in much the same way as a painting or a bunch of flowers. Lydgate sought in his wife 'that distinctive womanhood which must be classed with flowers and music' (Chapter 16), Sir James insisted that his wife become a perfect horsewoman, not for the skill or pleasure that it might give her but so 'that she may accompany her

*Letter to Charles Bray, 5 July 1884, in J. Cross, *George Eliot's Life*, Blackwood, London, 1885, p. 279.

husband' (Chapter 2). Should the husband fall ill, it was her duty to nurse him. As Mr Trumbull remarks: 'A man whose life is of any value should think of his wife as a nurse' (Chapter 37). Mr Casaubon married so as to secure 'the solace of female tendance for his declining years' (Chapter 7).

It is Mr Casaubon who provides us with a blueprint of what to look for in a woman when considering her for the position of wife, and he congratulates himself that 'Providence, in its kindness, has supplied him with the wife he needed' (Chapter 29). Whether Providence had taken equal care with Miss Brooke in presenting her with Mr Casaubon was an idea that could hardly have occurred to him. Knowing Mr Casaubon, we might be tempted to dismiss him as an exception, but George Eliot has no intention of letting her readers off so lightly. In a manner typical of her writing she moves from the particular to the general to indicate that this is not an opinion held by an eccentric and selfish individual but by the entire population. 'Society,' she writes, 'never made the preposterous demand that a man should think as much about his own qualifications for making a charming girl happy as he thinks of hers for making himself happy. As if a man could choose not only his wife but his wife's husband!' (Chapter 29).

One of the themes George Eliot discusses in *Middlemarch* is the dilemma of one possessed 'of a certain spiritual grandeur ill-matched with the meanness of opportunity' (Prelude). These words refer to Dorothea, and there can be little doubt that George Eliot thought also of her own struggle for an education and the right to participate in the intellectual life of the community when she created the character of Miss Brooke.

Dorothea stands out from the rest of the women in her society, she is the cygnet 'reared uneasily among the ducklings in the brown pond' (Prelude). She refuses to bow to fashion whether it be in hair style or manner of dress. She possesses a social conscience and longs to be free from the 'gentlewoman's oppressive liberty' (Chapter 28). Like John Bunyan's Christian, Dorothea asks the question, 'What shall I do?' (Chapter 28). But unlike him, she, because of her sex, is unable to pursue her quest; the constraints of society demand that it remains an 'inward vision' (Chapter 28). Her plain dress, her unwillingness to put herself out to please men, her intellectual aspirations, her religious fervour ('fasting like a Papist' (Chapter 1)), her concern for the poor and socially deprived, all of this leads to her being regarded with a certain degree of suspicion and apprehension, the argument against her being that of any conformist society against the non-conformist. 'Sane people did what their neighbours did' (Chapter 1).

Dorothea is mistrusted and feared by men and women alike. It is easy to see why the men, for example Lydgate and Mr Chichely, would adopt such an attitude because her refusal to conform to the role assigned to her by male society was a challenge to the notion of male superiority. The ordinary villagers would look askance at her because they lived by a code that had not changed for centuries; a code that was hierarchical and assigned to every person a place in the hierarchy— King over lord, lord over squire, squire over tenant farmer, and in all ranks male over female. But the women also express uneasiness about her. One example of this can be found in Chapter 56 when Mr Garth discusses Dorothea with Mrs Garth. He does not actually bestow the highest accolade a man could bestow on a woman, namely that she thinks and acts like a man, but the tone of his voice suggests this: 'She sees into things in that way.' Mrs Garth detects the tone: ' "But womanly, I hope," said Mrs Garth, half suspecting that Mrs Casaubon might not hold the true principle of subordination'. It is a tribute to George Eliot's insight into human nature that she sees that the women also fear the emancipated woman, for the very fact of her emancipation would bring home to other women the degree of their own subjugation. Such an insight might be commonplace today, but we must remember that *Middlemarch* was written in the 1860s when the feminist movement as we know it did not exist.

'Women were expected to have weak opinions' (Chapter 1), and the education they received, so scornfully described by Dorothea as 'that toy-box history of the world adapted to young ladies' (Chapter 10), often ensured that they did. 'Deep studies, classics, mathematics . . . are too taxing for a woman' (Chapter 7). She was not to concern herself with the affairs of the realm, for 'young ladies don't understand political economy' (Chapter 2). Should a woman possess intelligence, this still gave no cause for alarm for, as Lydgate pointed out, 'her knowledge is of a different sort' (Chapter 16). Sir James Chettam is aware of his own limitations and knows 'that his talents, even if let loose, would not set the smallest stream in the county on fire' (Chapter 2). He is also aware of the fact that Dorothea is intelligent, but this does not disturb him. Why not? Because 'A man's mind—what there is of it—has always the advantage of being masculine—as the smallest birch tree is of a higher kind than the soaring palm' (Chapter 2). The irony here is very obvious.

Patriarchy and colonisation

What is perhaps not quite so obvious is that George Eliot links patriarchal attitudes to colonisation, and places the woman in the role of the colonised. Just as the coloniser—here read male—regarded himself as superior to the colonised—here read female—so, too, did he regard his own flora as superior to the flora of the colonised lands. The result of this attitude was that generations of Africans, Australians, Canadians, and people from the Caribbean were to grow up despising their own landscape. When a character in a story by Jean Rhys (1894-1979) set in the Caribbean* suddenly declares that he hates both strawberries and daffodils, he is not simply rejecting a fruit and a flower. What he is rejecting is colonisation and the coloniser's insistence that the imported fruit and flower are superior to the indigenous. Again these may be commonplace issues today, but they were not so in the 1860s and it is a further illustration of George Eliot's insight.

To take up the question of irony. Throughout the novel, whenever the male/female relationship is discussed and the male assumes a patriarchal attitude, a note of irony creeps in. Take, for instance, the occasion when Dorothea makes an impassioned plea to her uncle to see how incongruous and hypocritical it would be for him to stand as a Reform candidate for Parliament when conditions on his own estate are so appalling. Will Ladislaw is also present, and we read: 'Will's admiration was accompanied with a chilling sense of remoteness. A man is seldom ashamed of feeling he cannot love a woman so well when he sees a certain greatness in her; nature having intended greatness for men' (Chapter 39). 'But,' George Eliot goes on to remark, 'Nature has sometimes made sad oversights in carrying out her intentions.'

It is in the Lydgate/Rosamond relationship that George Eliot most clearly exposes the fallacy of male superiority. One could argue that if Lydgate's pride was a flaw in his nature that was to lead to his downfall, so too was his ignorance of the true nature of women. Despite his intelligence and willingness to adapt to new methods in medicine, Lydgate displays the classic male attitude towards the woman. He rejects Dorothea because 'she did not look at things from a proper feminine angle' (Chapter 11), and he found it troublesome to talk to her because she was one of those women 'always wanting reasons, yet they are too ignorant to understand the merits of any question' (Chapter 10). Admittedly he was to change his mind but not before he was a much wiser and sadder man. He found Rosamond a much more suitable partner because she 'had just the kind of intelligence one would desire in a woman—polished, refined, docile' (Chapter 16). He believed in the superiority of the male to the female and in 'the innate submissiveness of the goose . . . to the strength of the gander' (Chapter 36).

In the end we find him willing to forgive the woman who has been

*Jean Rhys, 'The Day They Burned the Books', *Tigers are Better Looking*, André Deutsch, London, 1967.

responsible in so many ways for his downfall and for the destruction of his ambitions. Yet, even in the act of forgiveness he is still unable to think of this woman who has thwarted and frustrated him in every way, as an equal. 'It was inevitable,' we are told '. . . he should think of her as if she were an animal of another and feebler species' (Chapter 65). But, as the next sentence reminds us, 'Nevertheless she had mastered him'.

Dorothea and the question of tragedy

After having praised George Eliot's creation of Dorothea as 'the great achievement of the book', Henry James goes on to complain that 'Dorothea was altogether too superb a heroine to be wasted; yet she plays a narrower part than the imagination of the reader demands. She is of more consequence than the action of which she is the nominal centre.'*

But what Henry James seems to have forgotten was that George Eliot's aim was to present the story of 'the offspring of a certain spiritual grandeur ill-matched with the meanness of opportunity' (Prelude). In *Middlemarch*, George Eliot remains true to her purpose—to have presented Dorothea as Henry James would have wished would have been a betrayal of social reality.

We who live in the last decades of the twentieth century have come to accept that tragedy is not the preserve of the great and important. But we must remember that this has not always been the case and that the period in which George Eliot was writing was one which witnessed the cult of the hero—for instance, in Thomas Carlyle's *On Heroes, Hero Worship and the Heroic in History*.†

Henry James wondered if it was 'an unconscious instinct' or 'a deliberate plan' on George Eliot's part to present Dorothea as she did. George Eliot answers his query in *Middlemarch*. She predicts that six weeks after her marriage we are likely to find Dorothea weeping but that no one will find this tragic. For, she says:

> That element of tragedy which lies in the very fact of frequency, has not yet wrought itself into the coarse emotion of mankind; and perhaps our frames could hardly bear much of it. If we had a keen vision and feeling of all human life, it would be like hearing the grass grow and the squirrel's heart beat and we should die of that roar which lies on the other side of silence. As it is, the quickest of us walk about well wadded with stupidity (Chapter 20).

*Henry James, 'George Eliot's *Middlemarch*' in *A Century of George Eliot Criticism*, edited by G. S. Haight, Methuen, London, 1966, p. 82.
†Re-issued in 1970 by the University of Nebraska Press.

If her creation of Dorothea is one of her greatest achievements, so, too, is her realisation of the above truth. In her endeavour to reveal this truth to us 'she strips away a little of our "wadded stupidity" and enables us a little better to bear the burden of human reality'.*

Themes of illusion and disenchantment

The first obvious example of the theme of illusion can be seen in the marriages of Dorothea and Casaubon, and Rosamond and Lydgate. All four marry not for love but for selfish reasons, each believing the partner to be other than he or she is. All four come to regret their decisions and end up suffering under the yoke of marriage (Chapter 48).

What is perhaps of interest, given the times, is what degree of guilt, if any, can be attached to them for their choice of partner. Lydgate chose Rosamond as he would a flower or ornament for his home. Casaubon wanted a nurse and companion for his old age. Hardly admirable reasons for a choice of partner, but very conventional ones in that age. Both men expected their wives to be docile and submissive, and both were disappointed. But again, given the times and conventions of the period, one could only conclude that they were unfortunate. There is no doubt that Lydgate was naîve about women, but his expectations about what a wife should be were those of his own generation and of generations both before and after him. He may have been a radical about medical reform, but 'his tendency was not toward extreme opinions . . . he walked by hereditary habit' (Chapter 36).

Even Rosamond is conforming to the pattern of her particular social group in seeking a husband from a higher social stratum. 'It's a good British feeling to try and raise your family a little' (Chapter 13). The remark is Mr Vincy's but the sentiment was a general one at a time when the industrial middle-class was moving up the social ladder.

Let us turn to Dorothea. Marrying a man so that the world of learning which had previously been closed to you could be opened up, may again not be an ideal reason for choosing a partner; yet it is surely a much more admirable one than the others. It is not Dorothea whom George Eliot condemns but the society that has created the situation that leads Dorothea to marry Mr Casaubon. George Eliot states this quite explicitly in the Finale of the manuscript, and the Finale of the first published version which she revised for the 1874 edition. The first published version reads:

> Certainly those determining acts of her life were not totally beautiful. They were the mixed result of young and noble impulse

*W. J. Harvey, 'Idea and Image in the Novels of George Eliot' in *Critical Essays on George Eliot*, edited Barbara Hardy, Routledge and Kegan Paul, London, 1970, p. 198.

struggling under prosaic conditions. Among the many remarks passed on her mistakes, it was never said in the neighbourhood of Middlemarch that such mistakes could not have happened if the society into which she was born had not smiled on propositions of marriage from a sickly man to a girl less than half his own age—on modes of education which make a woman's knowledge another name for motley ignorance—on rules of conduct which are in flat contradiction with its own loudly asserted beliefs. While this is the social air in which mortals begin to breathe, there will be collisions such as those in Dorothea's life, where great feelings will take the aspect of error, and great faith the aspect of illusion.

Lack of space prevents further discussion about the reasons for George Eliot's revisions, but the reader is referred to Jerome Beaty who suggests that while the 1874 version may be more congenial to the modern sensibility, it does not suggest the moral vision of the novel as adequately as the earlier version.*

We could argue that George Eliot has her revenge on those who married for reasons that she would disaprove of though it is a high price that Lydgate pays for his insensitivity to the true merits of Dorothea. Dorothea is the only one who eventually finds happiness, a happiness that may not be commensurate with her ambitions, but a happiness no less.

There are other obvious instances of illusion and subsequent disillusionment in the novel†, for example, Fred's reliance on inheriting money, Mr Bulstrode's hope that his former life would not be revealed, Mr Casaubon's belief that he could discover the key to all mythologies. But the person who suffers the most tragic consequences because of illusion is Lydgate. He is arrogant enough to believe that he can control his own destiny. When we first meet him, he considers it 'a ridiculous piece of bad logic that he, with his unmixed resolutions of independence and his select purpose, would find himself . . . in the grasp of petty alternatives, each of which was repugnant to him' (Chapter 18). Yet, when we finally leave him, his life and work have been completely destroyed by others who 'had thrust themselves into his life and thwarted his purposes' (Chapter 73).

In his innocence Lydgate believed that if the cause was good then everything and everyone must remain subservient to it. What he failed to take into account was the all-powerful influence of money and the consequences when 'the scientific conscience [gets] into the debasing

---

*For a discussion of this issue see Jerome Beaty, 'The Text of the Novel: A Study of the Proof' and W. J. Harvey, 'Criticism of the Novel: Contemporary Reception'. Both essays appear in *Middlemarch: Critical Approaches to the Novel*, ed. by Barbara Hardy, Athlone Press, London, 1967.

†An interesting essay on this theme is Barbara Hardy's 'The Moment of Disenchantment in George Eliot's Novels' in *Review of English Studies*, V, 1954.

company of money obligation and selfish respects' (Chapter 73). Lydgate's dependence on Bulstrode is an individual instance of this, but in more general terms it is an excellent example of capitalism in its role of patron and the dangers inherent in this situation. It is no coincidence that Mr Bulstrode is a banker and that his principle was 'to gain as much power as possible' (Chapter 16).

The power of money is one of the things that is stressed throughout the novel. It is quite obvious that George Eliot despises 'money-craving, with all its base hopes' (Chapter 64); Dorothea was not one of Mr Trumbull's 'lady-birds' (Chapter 60), but in this matter, as in all others, the author acknowledges that the issue is not a simple one. As Mr Farebrother remarks, 'It's a rather strong check to one's self-complacency to find out how much of one's right doing depends on not being in want of money' (Chapter 63).

Character, circumstance and destiny

'Character,'—says Novalis, in one of his questionable aphorisms —'character is destiny'. But not the whole of our destiny.
The Mill on the Floss, VI, 6

Our deeds determine us, as much as we determine our deeds; and until we know what has been or will be the peculiar combination of outward with inward facts, which constitutes a man's critical actions, it will be better not to think ourselves wise about his character.
Adam Bede, Chapter 29

These quotations from two other novels by George Eliot point to the two shaping forces of a person's life and suggest the reciprocity that exists between them. It is true, of course, that people with strong wills may be more in command of their lives, but 'there is no creature whose inward being is so strong that it is not greatly determined by what lies outside it' (Finale). If Lydgate was naïve about women and money, he was even more so in his belief that he was strong enough to resist outside influences. What he failed to take into account was the interrelationship of each life with the others, to understand the truth of Mr Brooke's statement, ' "We're all one family, you know—it's all one cupboard" ' (Chapter 51). Very early in the novel George Eliot warns the reader that 'no man is an island':

But anyone watching keenly the stealthy convergence of human lots, sees a slow preparation of effects from one life on another, which tells like a calculated irony on the indifference or the frozen stare with which we look at our unintroduced neighbour. Destiny stands by sarcastic with our *dramatis personæ* folded in her hand. (Chapter 11)

The last statement suggests that her characters are completely determined. But this is not so. Their fate is determined, not only by circumstances but also by themselves. W. J. Harvey* has pointed out that George Eliot's vision of man as both free and yet determined accords well with the life-stage analogy and that her novels are full of imagery and other linguistic patterns which depend on the basic idea which is found in the opening lines of Jacques's speech in Shakespeare's play *As You Like It* (II.7.139–40):

> All the world's a stage
> And all the men and women merely players:

In terms of the life-stage analogy, the author in the role of omniscient narrator is the stage manager, the characters are the actors, and the readers the audience. The effect is to link life and literature and, by so doing, involve the reader in the world of the novel.

Whilst it is true that the actors' parts are written for them, it is also true that it depends on them how well they play their roles. It may be a limited freedom, but it exists. So, too, does the freedom to develop. Some of George Eliot's characters remain static, but not her major characters. She makes explicit reference to this in Chapter 15 when she is discussing Lydgate: 'Character too,' she says, 'is a process and an unfolding. The man was still in the making . . . and there were both virtues and faults capable of shrinking or expanding'.

George Eliot suggests that there can be another factor that influences us and so shapes our lives, and that is 'the saving influence of a noble nature' (Chapter 82):

> The presence of a noble nature, generous in its wishes, ardent in its charity, changes the lights for us: we begin to see things again in their larger, quieter masses, and to believe that we too can be seen and judged in the wholeness of our character. (Chapter 76)

This is Dorothea's achievement. Through *Middlemarch* it is also George Eliot's.

List of characters

Overleaf is a list in alphabetical order of all the characters who appear in *Middlemarch*. The principal characters are shown in capital letters and an asterisk alongside a character indicates that the character is discussed in some detail in Part 3. The number after each entry indicates the chapter in which the character first appears.

*W. J. Harvey, 'Idea and Image in the Novels of George Eliot' in *Critical Essays on George Eliot*, edited by Barbara Hardy, Routledge and Kegan Paul, London, 1970. In particular, see Section VII, pp. 184–98.

Abel, bailiff at Stone Court (69)

Abel, Mrs, Bulstrode's housekeeper at Stone Court (69)

Bagster, Mr, Whig M.P. for Middlemarch (38)

Ballard, Mrs, schoolmistress (40)

Bambridge, Mr, horse-dealer and money lender (23)

Blakesley, a Middlemarch judge (56)

Bowyer, Mr, an idle bachelor and ventriloquist (16)

Bretton, Mrs, the former owner of the Lydgates' house (36)

Briggs, Sir James Chettam's coachman (84)

BROOKE, Mr Arthur, country squire, uncle and guardian of Dorothea and Celia (1)

BROOKE, Celia, Dorothea's younger sister (1)

*BROOKE, Dorothea (Mrs Casaubon, Mrs Ladislaw), Mr Brooke's niece (1)

BULSTRODE, Mrs Harriet, Bulstrode's wife and Mr Vincy's sister (11)

Bulstrode, Kate and Ellen, daughters of the Bulstrodes (26)

BULSTRODE, Mr Nicholas, Middlemarch banker (10)

Bunch, a sheep-stealer (4)

Byles, a Middlemarch butcher (71)

Cadwallader, Mrs Elinor, wife of the vicar, a busybody (5)

Cadwallader, Reverend Humphrey, rector of Tipton and Freshitt (6)

Carter, Mrs, Mr Brooke's cook (6)

*CASAUBON, Reverend Edward, rector of Lowick, a self-centred scholar and pedant (1)

Chettam, the Dowager Lady, mother of Sir James (6)

Chettam, Arthur, Celia's baby son (49)

CHETTAM, Sir James, a prosperous landowner who marries Celia when Dorothea refuses him (1)

Chichely, Mr, coroner at Middlemarch (10)

Clemmens, Mr, of Brassing, the solicitor who draws up Featherstone's last will (35)

Clintup, Mr, a nurseryman (60)

Cooper, Timothy, farm labourer (56)

Crabbe, Mr, a Middlemarch glazier (71)

Cranch, Mrs Martha, Peter Featherstone's poor sister (32)

Cranch, Tom, Mrs Cranch's son (32)

Crowse, Mr, a curate (14)

Dagley, Mr, farmer on Mr Brooke's estate (38)

Dagley, Mrs, his overworked wife (39)

Dagley, Jacob, their little son (39)

Dibbits, Middlemarch druggist (45)

Dill, Middlemarch barber (71)

Dollop, Mrs, landlady of the Tankard (45)

Dover, Mr, a silversmith (58)

Downes, Kit, farmer on Mr Brooke's land (39)

Duncan, Archie, a spiteful admirer of Sarah Dunkirk (60)

Dunkirk, Mr, a dishonest London pawnbroker and Mr Bulstrode's early patron (61)

Dunkirk, Mrs, the pawnbroker's wife, who later marries Bulstrode

Dunkirk, Sarah, Will Ladislaw's mother and the Dunkirks' daughter (37)

Farebrother, Mrs, the vicar's mother (17)

FAREBROTHER, Reverend Camden, vicar of St Botolph's and later rector of Lowick (13)

Farebrother, Miss Winifred, the vicar's sister (17)

Faulkner, man to whom Bambridge sells horses (71)

Featherstone, Jonah, Peter's brother (32)

FEATHERSTONE, Peter, a rich miser, who owns Stone Court (11)

Featherstone, Joshua Rigg, Peter's natural son and Raffles's stepson who inherits Stone Court (35)

Featherstone, Solomon, Peter's brother (12)

Fitchett, Mrs, lodge-keeper at Tipton Grange (6)

Flavell, a Methodist preacher (39)

Ford, Hiram, a waggoner (56)

Gambit, Dr, a doctor (45)

Garth, Alfred, Mary's brother (24)

Garth, Ben, Mary's brother (24)

GARTH, Caleb, Mary's father; surveyor and estate manager. A very honest man (17)

Garth, Christy, Mary's eldest brother (40)

Garth, Jim, Mary's brother (40)

Garth, Letty, Mary's sister (24)

GARTH, Mary, the Garths' eldest daughter (11)

Garth, Mrs Susan, Caleb's wife (17)

Giles, an unsuccessful candidate for Parliament (38)

Grinsell, Lord, an acquaintance of the Dowager Lady Chettam (55)

Hackbutt, Mr, a Middlemarch tanner (18)

Hackbutt, Mrs, his wife (74)

Hackbutt, Fanny, one of Mrs Garth's pupils (24)

Hanmer, Mr, an engineer (24)

Hawley, Mr Frank, town-clerk of Middlemarch (18)

Hawley, young, a law student (66)

Hopkins, Mr, Middlemarch draper (36)

Horrock, Mr, a veterinarian (23)

John, Sir James Chettam's groom (3)

Joseph, Mr Trumbull's assistant (60)

Julia, Aunt, Mr Casaubon's aunt and Will Ladislaw's grand-mother (9)

Keck, editor of the Middlemarch *Trumpet* (38)

Kell, Mrs, housekeeper at Tipton Grange (62)

Kibble, silversmith at Brassing (36)

Ladislaw, Will's deceased father (37)

Ladislaw, Will's grandfather, a Polish refugee, who had married Mr Casaubon's Aunt Julia (37)

*LADISLAW, Will, Mr Casaubon's second cousin (9)

Larcher, Mrs, the carrier's wife (26)

Larcher, Caius, the carrier's son (27)

Larcher, Mr Edwin, carrier of Middlemarch (18)

Laure, Madame, a French actress who murdered her husband (15)

Lemon, Mrs, schoolmistress (11)

Lovegood, Sir James Chettam's farm-manager (3)

Lydgate, Captain, Sir Godwin's third son (58)

Lydgate, Sir Godwin, Tertius Lydgate's uncle (36)

*LYDGATE, Tertius, a young doctor who is anxious to try new medical methods (10)

Martha, Rosamond Lydgate's servant (77)

Mawmsey, Mr, Middlemarch grocer (45)

Medlicote, Lord, a patron of Mr Bulstrode's hospital (13)

Mengan, Mrs, Captain Lydgate's sister (58)

Minchin, Dr, a physician in Middlemarch (15)

Morgan, Miss, governess in the Vincy family (11)

Nash, Nancy, a charwoman whom Lydgate cures (45)

Naumann, Adolf, a German painter who has a studio in Rome, friend of Will Ladislaw (19)

Noble, Miss Henrietta, Mrs Farebrother's sister (17)

Oliver, a Middlemarch M.P. (38)

Peacock, Mr, Lydgate's pre-decessor in Middlemarch (11)

Pinkerton, Tory M.P. for Middlemarch (6)

Plymdale, Mr, a wealthy Middle-march manufacturer (11)

Plymdale, Ned, his son (27)

Plymdale, Mrs Selina, his wife (16)

Powderell, Mr, a retired

Middlemarch ironmonger (18)

Powderell, Mrs, the ironmonger's wife and one of Lydgate's patients (45)

Pratt, Mr Casaubon's butler (37)

Pritchard, servant in the Vincy family (11)

RAFFLES, John, Rigg Featherstone's stepfather, a drunkard and former business associate of Bulstrode's (41)

Renfrew, Mrs, one of Mr Brooke's dinner-party guests (10)

Sadler, a Middlemarch draper (36)

Sally, Mrs Garth's servant (24)

Simmons, Peter Featherstone's farm bailiff (14)

Spanning, Dr, an acquaintance of Mr Casaubon (37)

Spicer, Mr, shoemaker and Lowick parish clerk (70)

Spilkins, a foolish young man (60)

Sprague, Dr, senior physician of Middlemarch who opposes Lydgate's new ideas (15)

Sprague, Mrs, his wife (74)

Standish, Mr, Peter Featherstone's lawyer (10)

Strype, Mrs, washerwoman befriended by Bulstrode (16)

Taft, Mrs, Middlemarch lady who loves knitting (26)

Tantripp, Dorothea's maid (4)

Tegg, a shoemaker (16)

Thesiger, the Reverend Edward, rector of St Peter's, Middlemarch (18)

Toller, Mr, a medical practitioner in Middlemarch who dislikes both Lydgate and Bulstrode (15)

Toller, Mr Harry, a Middlemarch brewer (63)

Toller, Miss Sophy, his daughter who marries Ned Plymdale (64)

Toller, Mrs Tom, friend of Mrs Hackbutt (74)

Trawley, a friend of Lydgate's when he was a student (17)

Triton, Lord, a friend of Mrs Cadwallader (54)

Trumbull, Mr Borthrop, a Middlemarch auctioneer and second cousin of Peter Featherstone (32)

Tucker, Mr, Casaubon's middle-aged curate (9)

Tyke, the Reverend Walter, Middlemarch curate who is appointed hospital chaplain instead of Mr Farebrother (13)

Vigo, Mrs, the woman Dowager Lady Chettam thinks would be a good companion to Dorothea when Casaubon dies (54)

Vincy, Bob, second son of Mr and Mrs Vincy (11)

VINCY, Fred, eldest son of Mr and Mrs Vincy (11)

Vincy, Louisa, Fred's little sister (16)

Vincy, Mrs Lucy, wife of Mr Vincy (11)

VINCY, Rosamond, the Vincys' eldest daughter who marries Lydgate (10)

Vincy, Mr Walter, mayor of Middlemarch (10)

Waule, Mrs Jane, Featherstone's greedy sister (12)

Waule, John, her son (12)

Wrench, Mr, doctor who attended the Vincy family and who is replaced by Lydgate (11)

Part 4

Hints for study

FIRST SOME WORDS OF ADVICE which apply not only to *Middlemarch* but to a study of any work of literature.

The first piece of advice is given by Dr Johnson (1709–84), who is regarded as one of the greatest of all English writers. The reader he says, should

> read on through brightness and obscurity . . . . Let him preserve his comprehension of the dialogue and his interest in the story, and when the pleasures of novelty have ceased, let him attempt exactness and read the commentators. Particular passages are cleared by notes, but the general effect of the work is weakened. The mind is refrigerated by interruption; the thought is diverted from the principal subject; the reader is weary, he suspects not why; and at last throws away the book which he has so diligently studied.

Dr Johnson is saying that the first time you read a book you should try to read it without referring to notes or critical works on it. You may occasionally have to look at your dictionary but you should try to use it as little as possible during the first reading. Usually the meaning of the passage is clear even if there are one or two words you may not know. If you are constantly stopping to look up words and notes, you will not only fail to follow the story properly, but, what is worse, you are most likely to come to hate the novel, so that from being something that can delight as well as teach, it will become an instrument of torture. And this is not the intention.

The second piece of advice is that you should try first of all to work out your own ideas before you read any criticism. And if you find you do not agree with what the critic says you should not immediately change your point of view. Instead you should examine the point more carefully and try to find out why you differ. Having done this, you may then decide to change your own opinion. This does not matter. What matters is that you have given careful thought to the issues involved. This approach will lead you to a much more thoughtful and thorough performance.

The third piece of general advice concerns the method of studying. Some people will have one method of studying a text, others a quite different one. There is no one correct method. The following hints, therefore, although they are made from experience and have all been well tried in practice, represent only one way of studying *Middlemarch*. You may have another.

Suggested study method

The following three stages in studying *Middlemarch* are suggested:

First of all, before starting on the *Preliminary Reading*, look through Part 2, A general summary.

---

1. Preliminary reading

The amount of time that you are able to spend on studying *Middlemarch* obviously matters greatly. Even if, however, your time is very limited, you are still most strongly advised to start by reading quickly through all the book. What points should be borne in mind at this stage?

(*a*) Try to get a general idea of the plot, that is, what happens in the book.

(*b*) Find out who the main characters are and get at least a broad idea of the personalities *without* going into details as yet.

(*c*) Who are the minor characters? What part do they play in the plot? For example, what part does John Raffles play in the plot? Why is it important that Mr Bambridge is a horse-dealer?

(*d*) Try to remember—but again not in detail—the main sequence of events.

(*e*) Try to form a very general impression of the relationships between the main characters. What is the relationship between Dorothea and Lydgate? What is the relationship between Dorothea and Rosamond? What parallels does George Eliot draw between them?

(*f*) What do you think of the minor characters?

(*g*) What do you think is the main theme of the novel? Are there minor themes as well? Does the author have a message, and if she does, what is that message?

(*h*) What is the setting? Does the setting change? Does the setting tell us anything in particular? Does it help to explain the theme?

When you have finished this quick preliminary reading, it is a good idea, after you have closed the book, to think a little now about your general impressions. You could also try to note them down. Having done this, you *should* have:

(1) a general outline of the plot

(2) a general idea of the main characters and, possibly, a more vague idea of the minor ones

(3) a general idea of what the author is trying to tell the reader.

You are now ready for the next major stage.

2. Detailed reading

Before going on to this stage you should

(a) read through Part 1, The life of George Eliot. This will give you some idea of what the author was like and some clues perhaps to what she believed in and wanted to teach.

(b) Read through the *whole* of Part 3, Commentary, to get a general idea of the themes and characters in the book, and of its structure.

(c) Prepare the outline of a master sheet which you will fill in as you read the story for the second time. The master sheet should be divided into sections, each of them representing a major aspect of the novel, and each sub-divided into subsections. For *Middlemarch* the following sections and subsections might be selected:

Major characters (Dorothea; Casaubon; Ladislaw; Lydgate; Rosamond; Bulstrode; Mr Brooke; Celia)

Chief themes (Disenchantment; Character and destiny; Role of women; The use of irony; The power of money)

The novel as documentation (Political background; Social distinctions, Religion; Attitude to medicine)

Divide each section into columns under the appropriate headings for the subsections. Thus for *Chief themes* the following column headings might be used: Disenchantment; Character and destiny; Role of women; The use of irony, The power of money. You might wish to alter or omit some of the subsection headings suggested above, or add new ones, according to your own view of the novel.

Once you have prepared your master sheet, read the book for the second time, and each time you come across a particularly important passage which is relevant to any of the sections in your master sheet, make a note of it under the appropriate subsection heading. (You will find that on occasions the same passage will be relevant to several sections.) It is up to you whether you note down the page reference only or follow it with a brief quotation for easy identification.

For instance, under Disenchantment you would probably note:

113. For the first time (Dorothea)

210. For the first time (Lydgate)

(The page numbers given here are those of the Penguin edition.)

When you have completed the second reading of the book you will have: (i) an overall picture of the main points, (ii) a convenient arrangement of these points under separate headings for ready reference.

When material is collected on such a master sheet it is much easier to see the implications that you might miss if the special points are not singled out and collected, and trace the development of a theme. For example, the master sheet enables you to trace Dorothea's gradual disillusionment with Mr Casaubon, the role played by money, the role of women in that period, the attitude to medicine, and so on.

A. Summaries

You have now established the general outlines and you have prepared your master sheet so that you know what points you are looking at in particular. The time has come for a thorough, careful and close reading of the text. You should read the book chapter by chapter, and consult the glossary and notes to each chapter in Part 2, Detailed summaries. Moreover, *you* should write out your own summary of each chapter. The process of making your own summary and thus of getting to know the book, thoroughly and completely, is, without any qualification whatever, the most useful thing you can do. Gaining this familiarity is, quite simply, the necessary condition for any further study of the text. Your own summary may differ from the one in these Notes. You may have included more points. This does not matter at all; on the other hand, your summary should *also* include the points in these Notes.

B. Commentary

You should also make your own commentary. Check the points in your own commentary with the commentaries in Part 2. If necessary, supplement your own commentary by including points from these. In addition you should select quotations in order to substantiate your points.

One of the most important things to learn before taking any examination or writing any essay is not to depart so far from the text that what *you* say has little connection with what the *author* of the book has written. Hence there is a need to be able to choose an appropriate quotation and thus to give the grounds on which you are establishing your argument.

C. Questions

You should now have a good idea of what happens in the story and what points matter. You should then write down what questions you think apply to each chapter and see if you can answer them.

---

3. Final revision

Quickly read through the book once more, comparing it with those notes, summaries, commentary and quotations which you have by now built up. The aim at this stage is that your attention should be concentrated upon *these*.

Before taking an examination or writing an essay read through all your notes and your other material. You should by now have become so familiar with the book that you only need to refer to it now and again to check or develop a point in your notes. These have now become the most important thing for you.

During an examination or writing an essay divide your work into four stages.

(1) Write down on a piece of paper as fast as possible the ideas that come to you immediately after you have read the question.
(2) Arrange these ideas in a coherent order so that your discussion develops clearly and logically. Plan your opening and your conclusion with particular care.
(3) Write your answer out in full.
(4) Read through your answer, check your argument, your language, your punctuation, your spelling, your syntax, and so on. This final stage should *on no account* be omitted.

Since time is one of the most essential factors, be continually aware of this. A rough and sensible division of the time you spend on these four stages would be as follows: (1) 20%, (2) 20%, (3) 50%, (4) 10%.

Key quotations

Below is a list of key quotations. The list is not inclusive. You may have others you wish to include because you find them significant. The quotations have been chosen:

(1) to help you to recall a particular point and to imprint it on your memory,
(2) to prevent you from digressing too far from the text.

You will find that as these are key quotations most of them are likely to occur on your master sheet. You should be able to identify each quotation, the speaker, the circumstances and the significance of the quotation.

All quotations are taken from the Penguin edition.

1. Here and there a cygnet is reared uneasily among the ducklings in the brown pond, and never finds the living stream in fellowship with its own oary-footed kind. Here and there is born a Saint Theresa, foundress of nothing, whose loving heart-beats and sobs after an unattained goodness tremble off and are dispersed among hindrances, instead of centering in some long-recognizable deed. (Prelude, p.26)

2. You always see what nobody else sees; it is impossible to satisfy you; yet you never see what is quite plain. (Chapter 4, p. 59)

3. For in that part of the country, before Reform had done its notable part in developing the political consciousness, there was a clearer distinction of ranks and a dimmer distinction of parties; so that Mr Brooke's miscellaneous invitations seemed to belong to that general laxity which came from his inordinate travel and habit of taking too much in the form of ideas. (Chapter 10, p. 115)

4. She did not look at things from the proper feminine angle. The society of such women was about as relaxing as going from your work to teach the second form, instead of reclining in a paradise with sweet laughs for bird-notes, and blue eyes for a heaven. (Chapter 11, p. 122)

5. But any one watching keenly the stealthy convergence of human lots, sees a slow preparation of effects from one life on another, which tells like a calculated irony on the indifference or the frozen stare with which we look at our unintroduced neighbour. Destiny stands by sarcastic with our *dramatis personæ* folded in her hand. (Chapter 11, p. 122)

6. I at least have so much to do in unravelling certain human lots, and seeing how they were woven and interwoven, that all the light I can command must be concentrated on this particular web, and not dispersed over that tempting range of relevancies called the universe. (Chapter 15, p. 170)

7. It would have seemed beforehand like a ridiculous piece of bad logic that he, with his unmixed resolutions of independence and his select purpose, would find himself at the very outset in the grasp of petty alternatives, each of which was repugnant to him. (Chapter 18, p. 210)

8. . . . we begin by knowing little and believing much, and we sometimes end by inverting the quantities. (Chapter 20, p. 227)

9. It was a hundred to one that some good chance would fall in his way; the longer he thought of it, the less possible it seemed that he should not have a good chance, and the less reasonable that he should not equip himself with the powder and shot for bringing it down. (Chapter 23, p. 268)

10. Mr Casaubon had never had a strong bodily frame, and his soul was sensitive without being enthusiastic: it was too languid to thrill out of self-consciousness into passionate delight; it went on fluttering in the swampy ground where it was hatched, thinking of its wings and never flying. (Chapter 29, p. 313)

11. Scenes which make vital changes in our neighbours' lot are but the background of our own, yet, like a particular aspect of the fields and trees, they become associated for us with the epochs of our own history, and make a part of that unity which lies in the selection of our keenest consciousness. (Chapter 34, p. 360)

12. This implicit reasoning is essentially no more peculiar to evangelical belief than the use of wide phrases for narrow motives is peculiar to Englishmen. There is no general doctrine which is not capable of eating out our morality if unchecked by the deep-seated habit of direct fellow-feeling with individual fellow-men. (Chapter 61, p. 668)

13. In the British climate there is no incompatibility between scientific insight and furnished lodgings: the incompatibility is chiefly between scientific ambition and a wife who objects to that kind of residence.' (Chapter 67, p. 732)

14. Who can know how much of his most inward life is made up of the thoughts he believes other men to have about him, until that fabric of opinion is threatened with ruin? (Chapter 68, p. 741)

15. It is curious what patches of hardness and tenderness lie side by side in men's dispositions. (Chapter 69, p. 753)

16. There is no sorrow I have thought more about than that—to love what is great, and try to reach it, and yet to fail. (Chapter 76, p. 821)

17. The pitiable lot is that of the man who could not call himself a martyr even though he were to persuade himself that the men who stoned him were but ugly passions incarnate—who knows that he is stoned, not for professing the Right, but for not being the man he professed to be. (Chapter 85, p. 881)

18. Certainly those determining acts of her life were not ideally beautiful. They were the mixed result of a young and noble impulse struggling amidst the conditions of an imperfect social state, in which great feelings will often take the aspect of error, and great

faith the aspect of illusion. For there is no creature whose inward being is so strong that it is not greatly determined by what lies outside it.   (Finale, p. 896)

Revision questions

If you know your text well and have read the commentary at the end of each chapter in Part 2, as well as Part 3 of these Notes, you should be able to answer all these questions.

1. What do you consider to be the major theme of *Middlemarch*?
2. Contrast Dorothea and Celia. Which of the two sisters sees more clearly? What is the relationship between clear-sightedness and virtue?
3. Discuss the theme of illusion and reality.
4. Show how George Eliot uses contrasting characters to emphasise the weaknesses and strengths of the respective characters.
5. What parallels can be drawn between Dorothea and Lydgate?
6. 'He [Mr Casaubon] was all she had at first imagined him to be: almost everything he had said seemed like a specimen from a mine, or the inscription on the door of a museum.' In what way is this an example of tragic irony? Give two other examples of tragic irony to be found in the book.
7. Give instances of water/dryness imagery in the novel and discuss their significance.
8. In what way does George Eliot use setting a) to create atmosphere, b) to tell us something about one or more of the characters? Give at least two examples of this technique.
9. What picture does the novel give of the role and status of women at that time?
10. Discuss *Middlemarch* as a social and political document.
11. Discuss the role played by money in the novel.
12. What is the function of the author's direct comments (authorial instrusion)?
13. If George Eliot is often ironical at the expense of her characters she is also compassionate towards them. Discuss this combination of irony and compassion and give examples of it.
14. In what way is the truth of the statement 'No man is an island' illustrated in the novel?
15. Discuss the theme of disenchantment.
16. What is the role played by the minor characters?
17. Discuss George Eliot's method of interweaving the various themes and plots.

Part 5

Suggestions for further reading

The text

Middlemarch, edited by W. J. Harvey, Penguin English Library, Penguin Books, Harmondsworth, 1965.

Other works by George Eliot

Scenes of Clerical Life, 1857 (stories)
Adam Bede, 1859 (novel)
'The Lifted Veil', 1859 (story)
Silas Marner, 1861 (novel)
Romola, 1863 (novel)
'Brother Jacob', 1864 (story)
Felix Holt the Radical, 1866 (novel)
The Spanish Gypsy, 1868 (poem)
The Legend of Jubal and Other Poems, 1874 (poems)
Daniel Deronda, 1876 (novel)
Impressions of Theophrastus Such, 1879 (essays)

Biography and Criticism

ADAM, IAN (ED.): *This Particular Web: Essays on 'Middlemarch'*, University of Toronto Press, Toronto, 1975. A collection of critical essays by leading George Eliot scholars. Various aspects of the novel are discussed, particularly its structure and its approach to character.

ANDERSON, QUENTIN: 'George Eliot in *Middlemarch*' in *From Dickens to Hardy*, Pelican Guide to English Literature, edited by Boris Ford, Penguin Books, Harmondsworth, 1958. This essay discusses *Middlemarch* and George Eliot's position among the other novelists of the period.

BEATY, JEROME: *'Middlemarch' from Notebook to Novel: a Study of George Eliot's Creative Method*, University of Illinois Press, Urbana, 1960. A very detailed discussion of the composition of

Middlemarch based on George Eliot's letters and journals, the notebook she kept while writing the novel, the *Middlemarch* manuscript, and the corrected proof of the first editions of the book, showing how *Middlemarch* was a fusion of two separate novels. It is a discussion not only of *Middlemarch* but also of George Eliot's creative method.

BEATY, JEROME: 'History by Indirection: the Era of Reform in *Middlemarch*' in *Victorian Studies*, 1,2, December, 1957, pp. 173–91. This article traces all the historical references in the novel and dates them.

BENNETT, JOAN: *George Eliot: Her Mind and Her Art*, Cambridge University Press, Cambridge, 1949. The first section of this book is concerned with George Eliot's life and its relevance to her work. It is a valuable introduction to the second section which examines her art as a novelist.

CAROLL, DAVID: 'Unity through Analogy: An interpretation of *Middlemarch*' in *Victorian Studies*, II, 1959. Points out the parallels between the development and fate of various characters. David Caroll also has an essay in *This Particular Web*.

CECIL, LORD DAVID: *Early Victorian Novelists*, Constable, London, 1934; Fontana, London, 1970. This deals not only with George Eliot but also with the other Victorian novelists and discusses George Eliot's place in the development of the novel.

COOPER, LETTICE: *George Eliot*, Longman, London, 1951. A very brief but informative introduction to George Eliot's life and works.

DAICHES, DAVID: *George Eliot: Middlemarch* (Studies in English Literature Series, No. 11), Edward Arnold, London, 1977. A general introduction to the work designed to provide in Coleridge's terms an aid to reflection for those who have already read the novel.

HAIGHT, GORDON S. (ED.): *A Century of George Eliot Criticism*. Methuen, London, 1966. A selection of criticism on George Eliot covering a period of one hundred years.

HAIGHT, GORDON S. (ED.): *The George Eliot Letters*, 9 vols, Yale University Press, New Haven, 1952–6. This is the most valuable source of information about George Eliot's life and her ideas.

HARDY, BARBARA: *The Novels of George Eliot*, Oxford University Press, New York, 1967. Contains individual chapters on each of the novels.

HARDY, BARBARA (ED.): *Critical Essays on George Eliot*, Routledge and Kegan Paul, London, 1970. Contains an essay on *Middlemarch*, '*Middlemarch*: a note on George Eliot's Wisdom'.

HARDY, BARBARA (ED.): *Middlemarch: Critical Approaches to the Novel*, Athlone Press, London, 1967. A collection of essays on *Middlemarch* by the major English and American scholars of

George Eliot. Presents a variety of approaches pointing to the greatness and diversity of the novel and instead of reaching one conclusion looks to an openness of response.

HARDY, BARBARA: *The Novels of George Eliot*, Athlone Press, London, 1959. Contains individual chapters on each of the novels using the 'new criticism' method.

JAMES, HENRY: 'George Eliot's *Middlemarch*' in *A Century of George Eliot Criticism*, edited by Gordon S. Haight, Methuen, London, 1966. An article on George Eliot's masterpiece by another great novelist.

LASKI, MARGHANITA: *George Eliot and Her World*, Thames and Hudson, London, 1973. Contains 123 illustrations and these, together with the text, make an excellent book on the subject.

LEAVIS, F. R.: *The Great Tradition*, Chatto and Windus, London, 1948. One of the most influential books written on the English novel. It contains studies of George Eliot, Henry James, and Joseph Conrad.

THALE, JEROME: *The Novels of George Eliot*, Columbia University Press, New York, 1959. Places George Eliot and her novels within the tradition of the English novel.

WILLEY, BASIL: *Nineteenth Century Studies: Coleridge to Matthew Arnold*, Chatto and Windus, London, 1955. An excellent study of the ideas of the nineteenth century and George Eliot's place in them.

The author of these notes

ANNA RUTHERFORD is a graduate of the University of Newcastle, New South Wales. She has taught in Australia, England and America, and, since 1966, in Denmark, where she is in charge of Commonwealth Studies at Aarhus University. She is Chairman of the European Branch of the Association for Commonwealth Literature and Language Studies, editor of *Kunapipi* and director of Dangaroo Press.

Her published works include *Common Wealth*; she is co-editor, with Donald Hannah, of *Commonwealth Short Stories*, and, with Kirsten Holst Petersen, of *Enigma of Values*, a work of criticism on the Guyanese writer Wilson Harris, and of *Cowries and Kobos: the West African Oral Tale, and Short Story*. She is also the author of the York Notes on *Silas Marner*.